Beautiful Birds Coloring Book For Adults

This Coloring book belongs to:

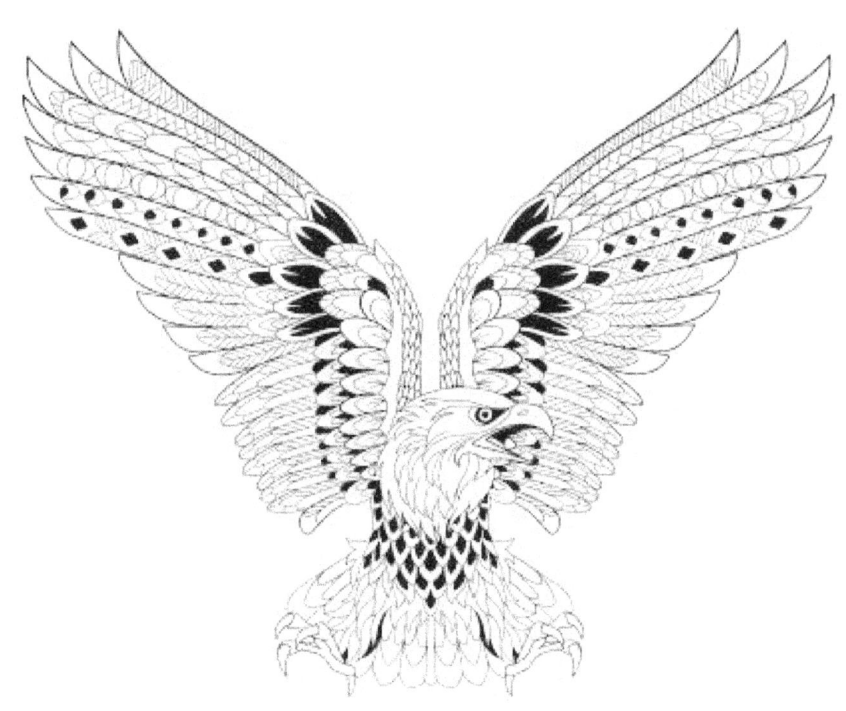

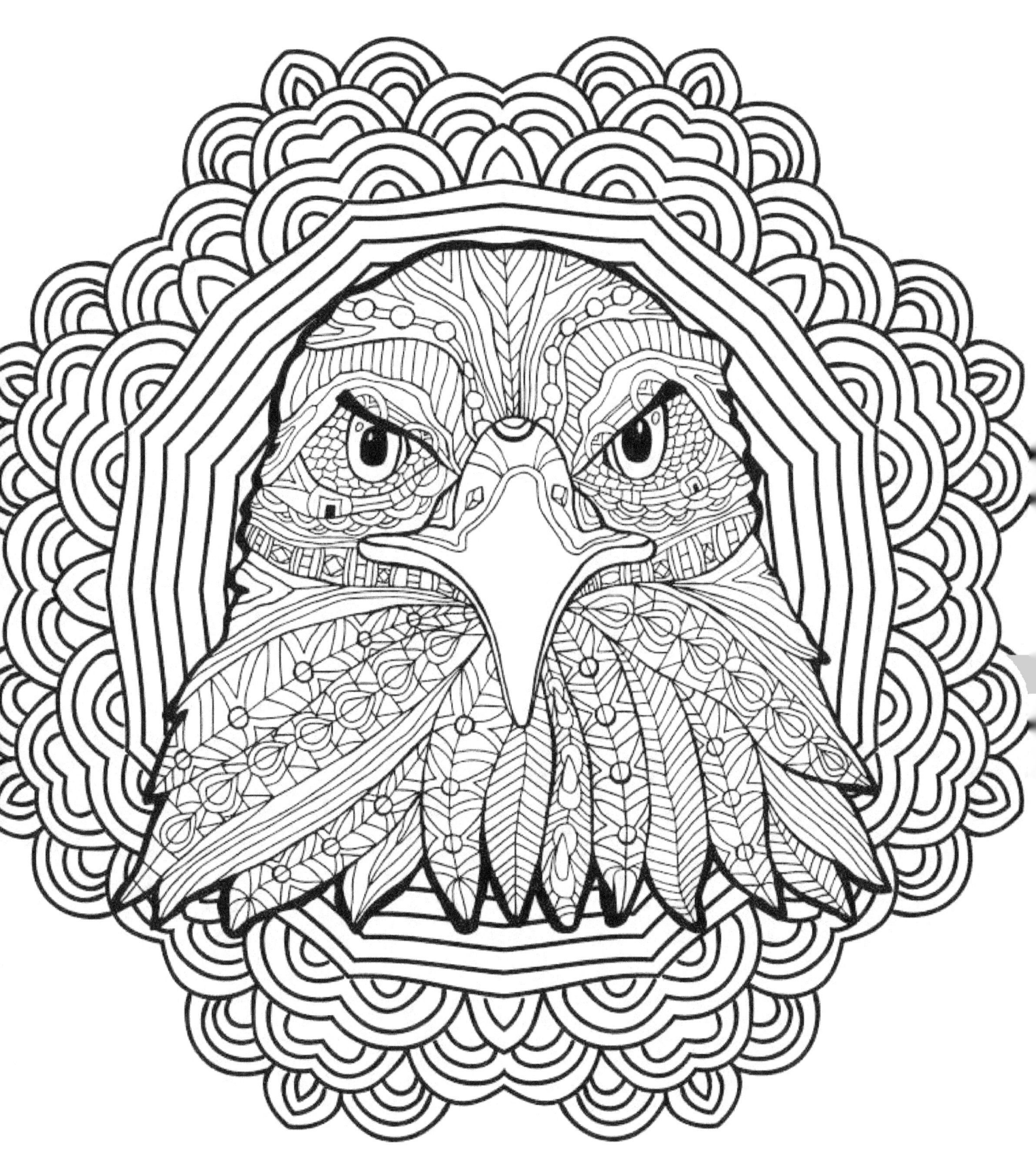

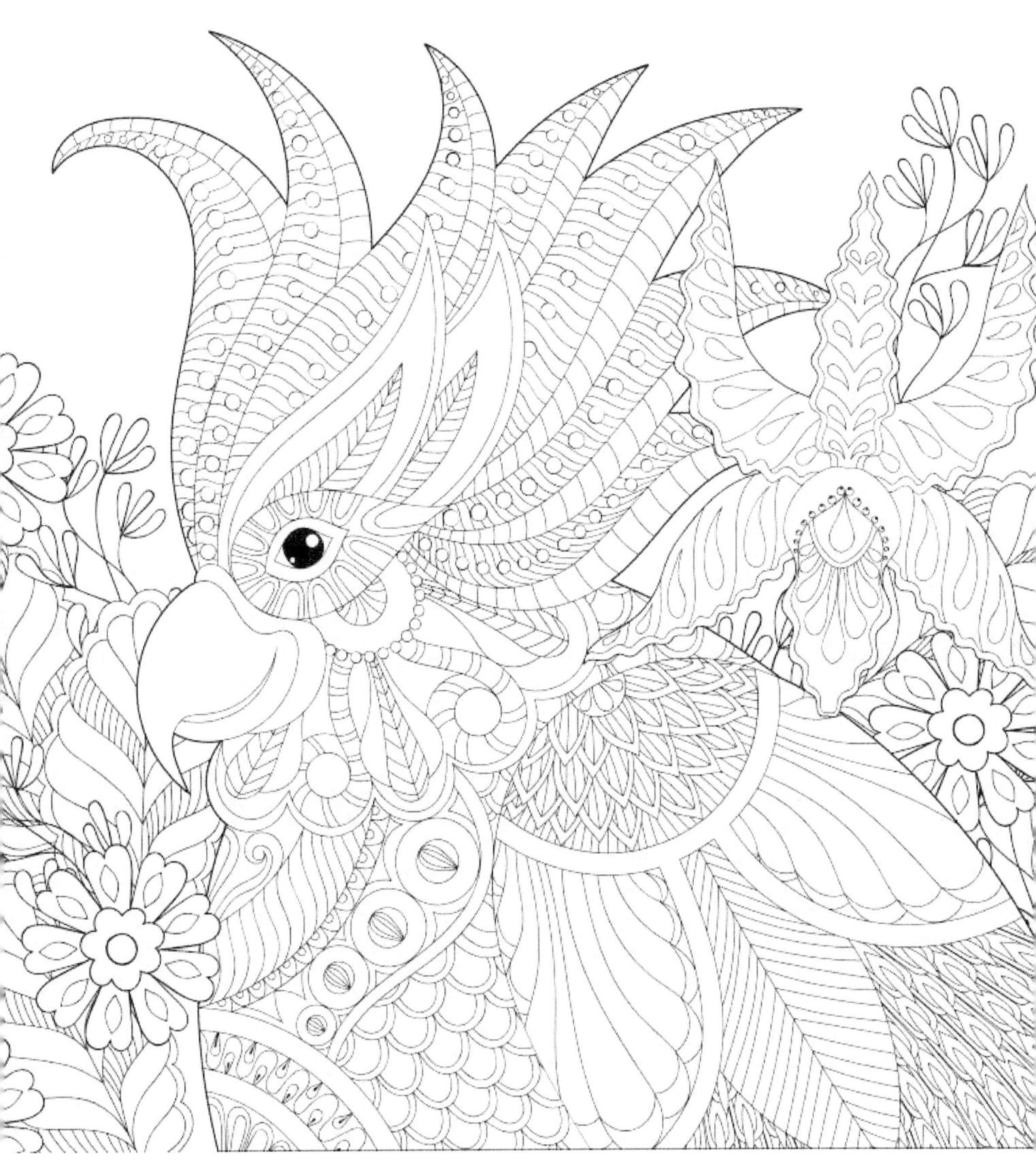

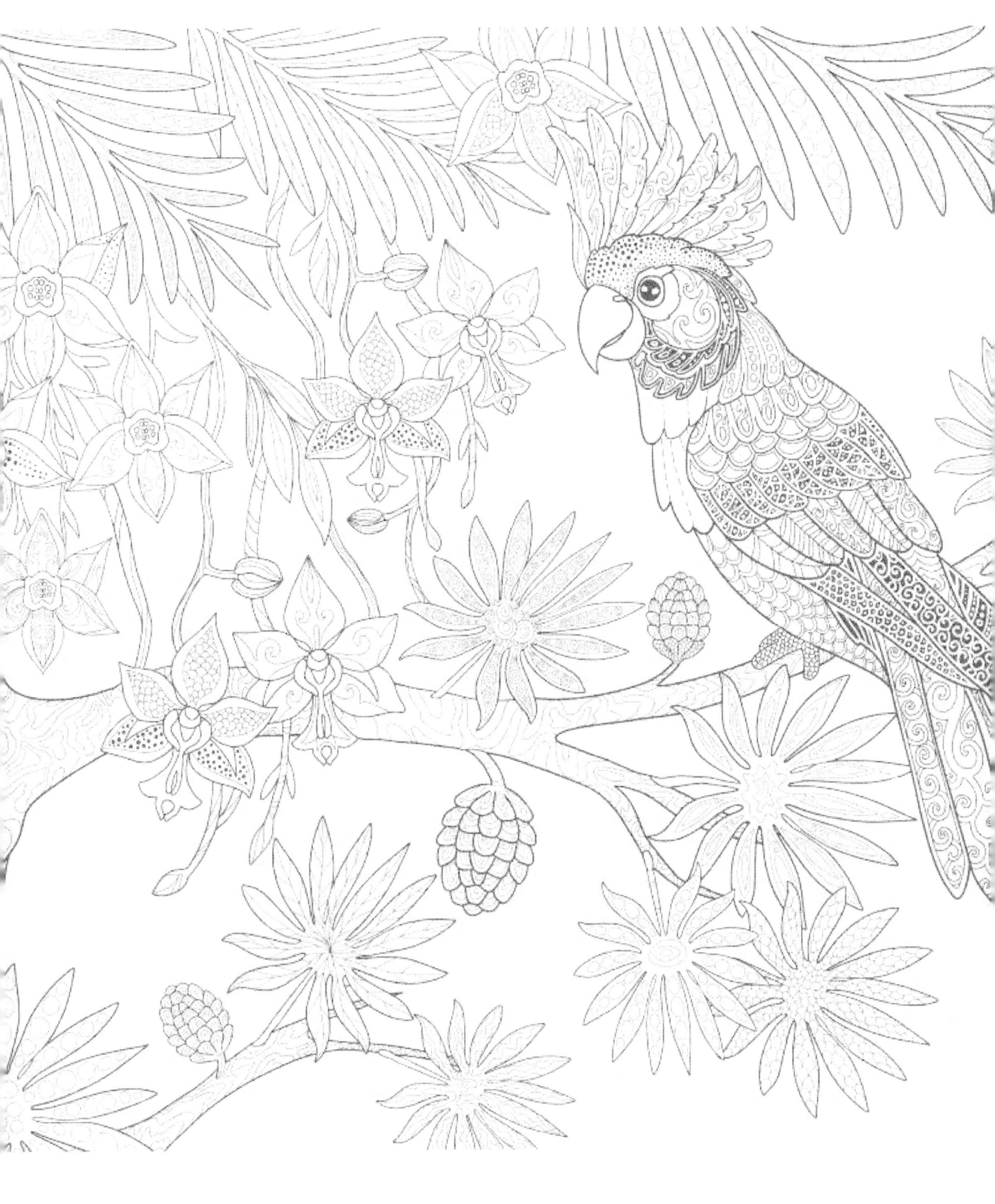

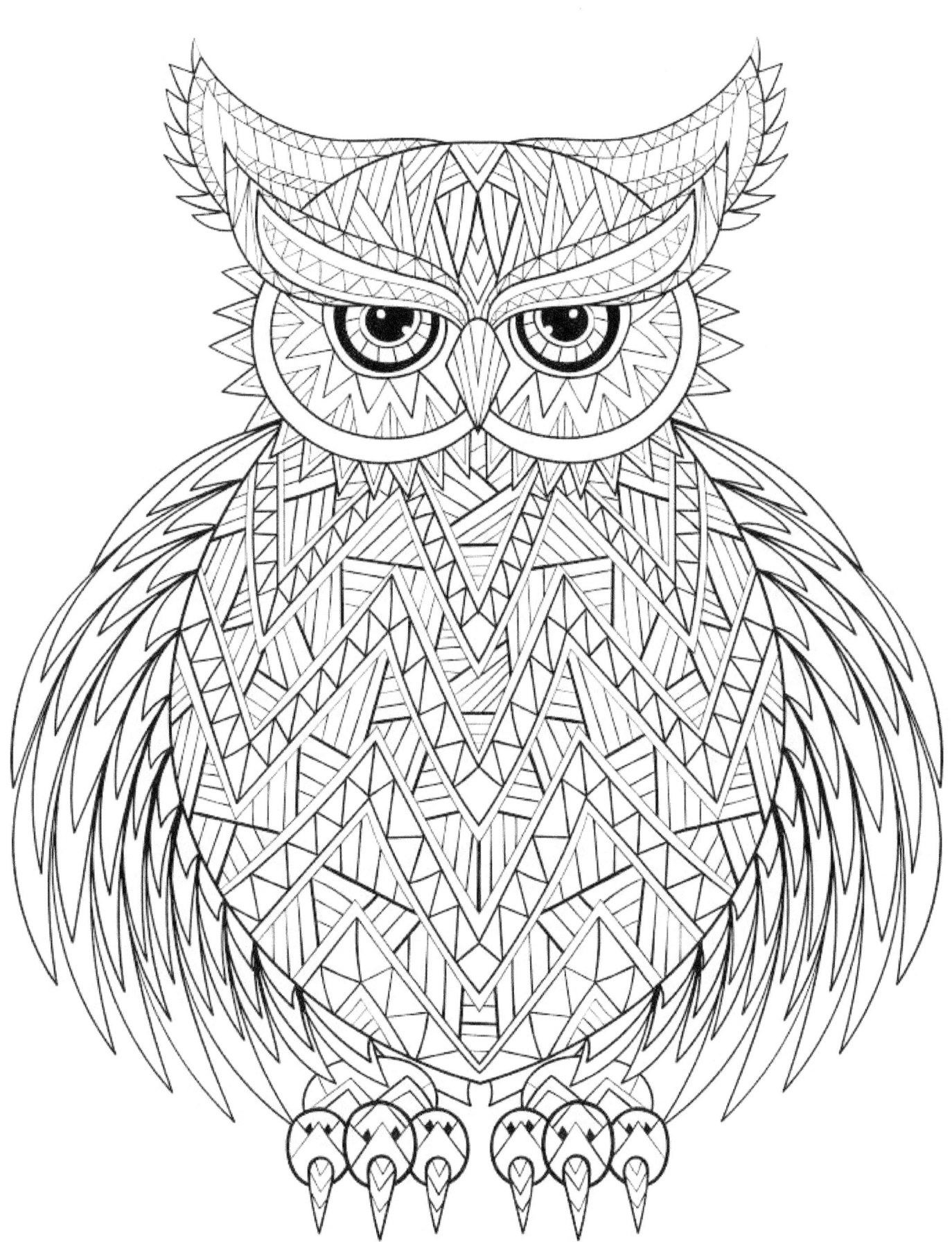

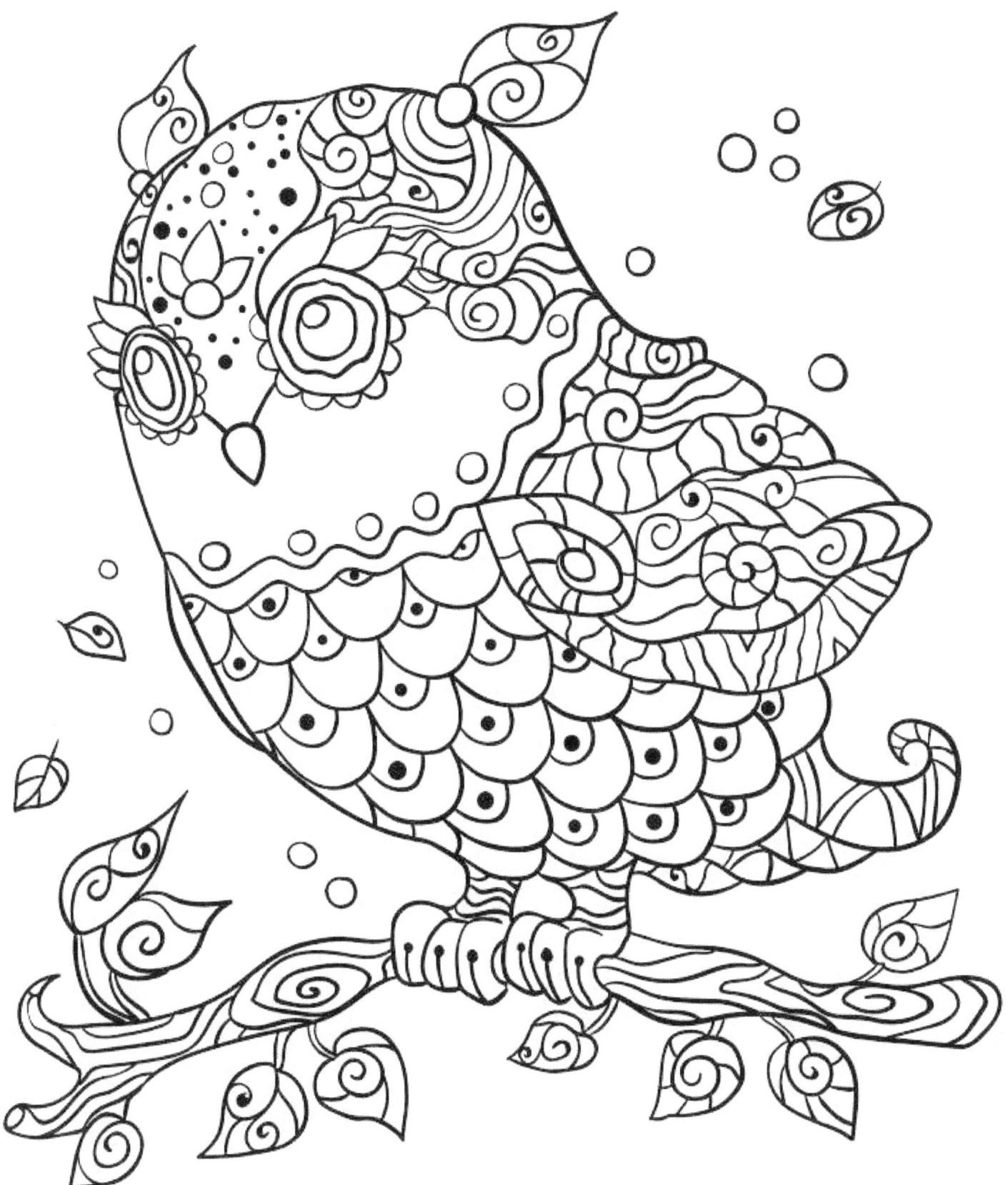

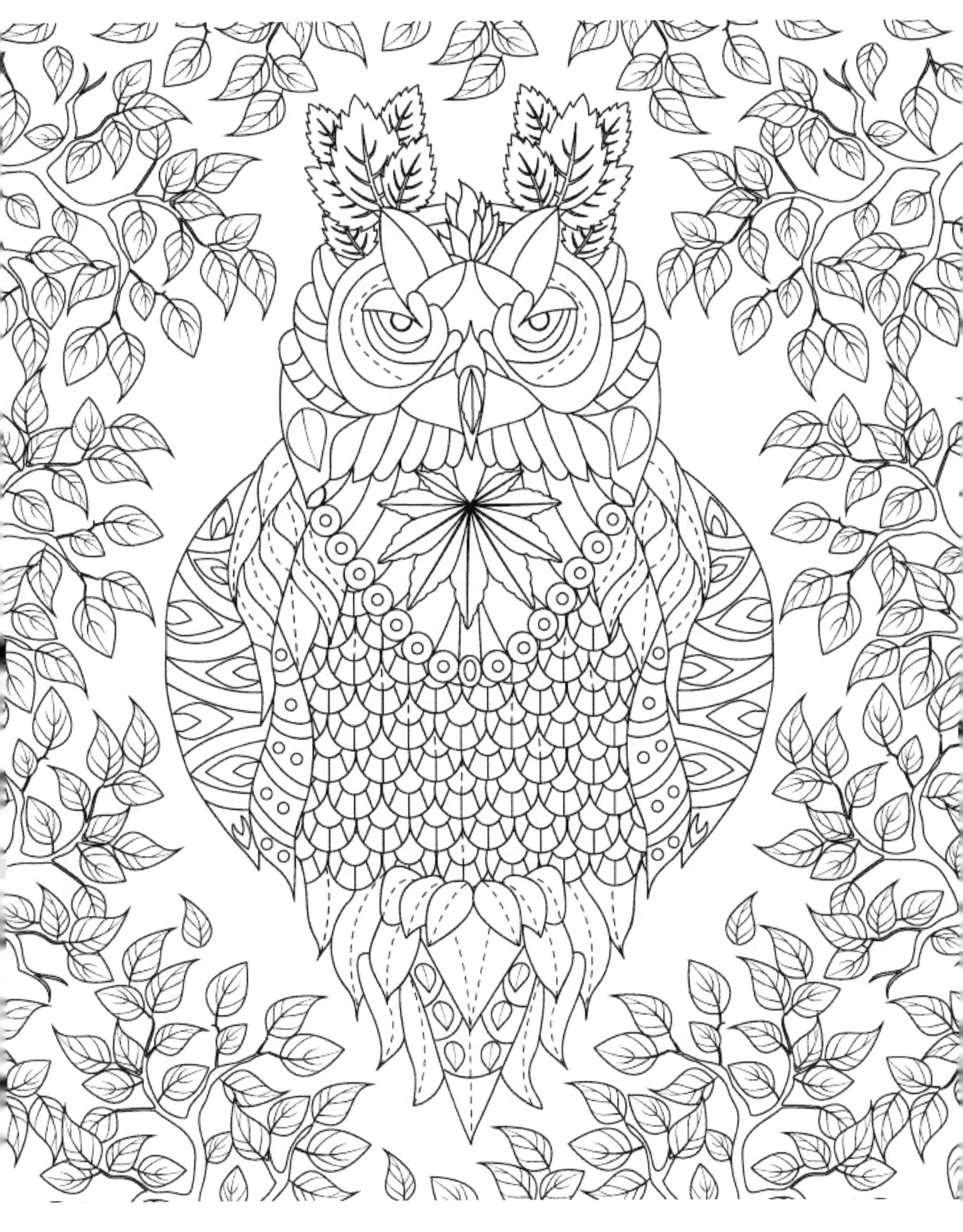

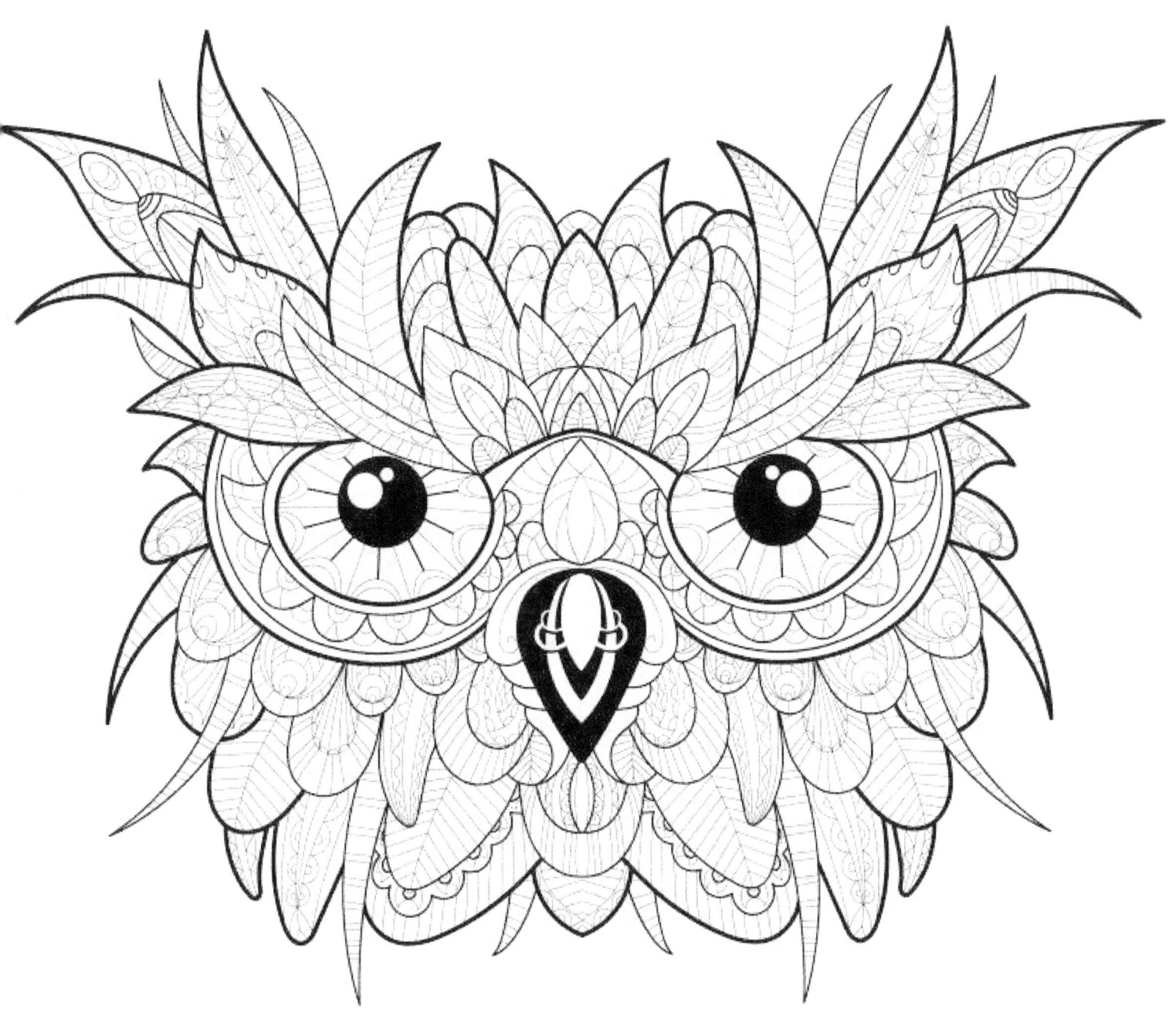

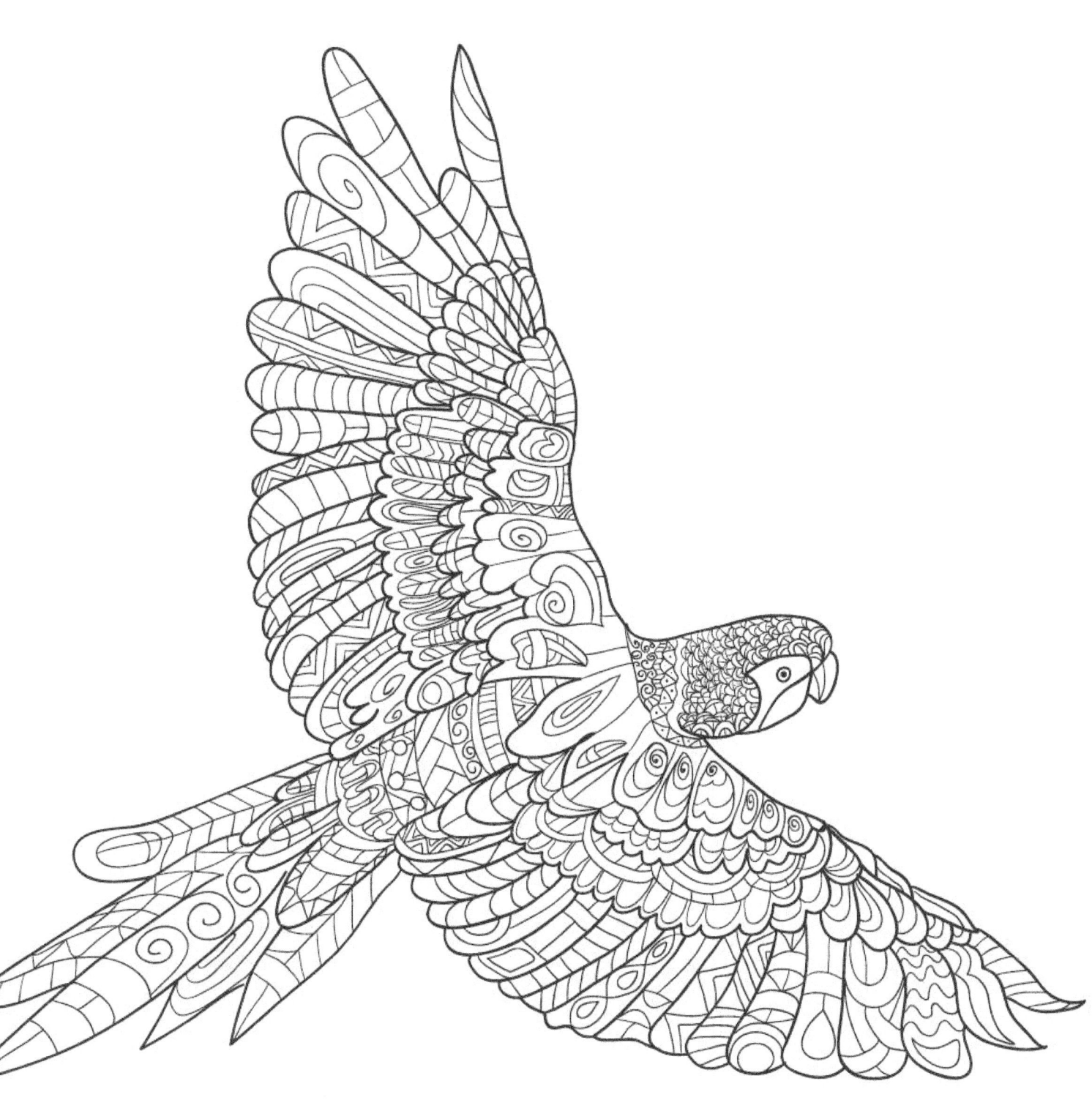

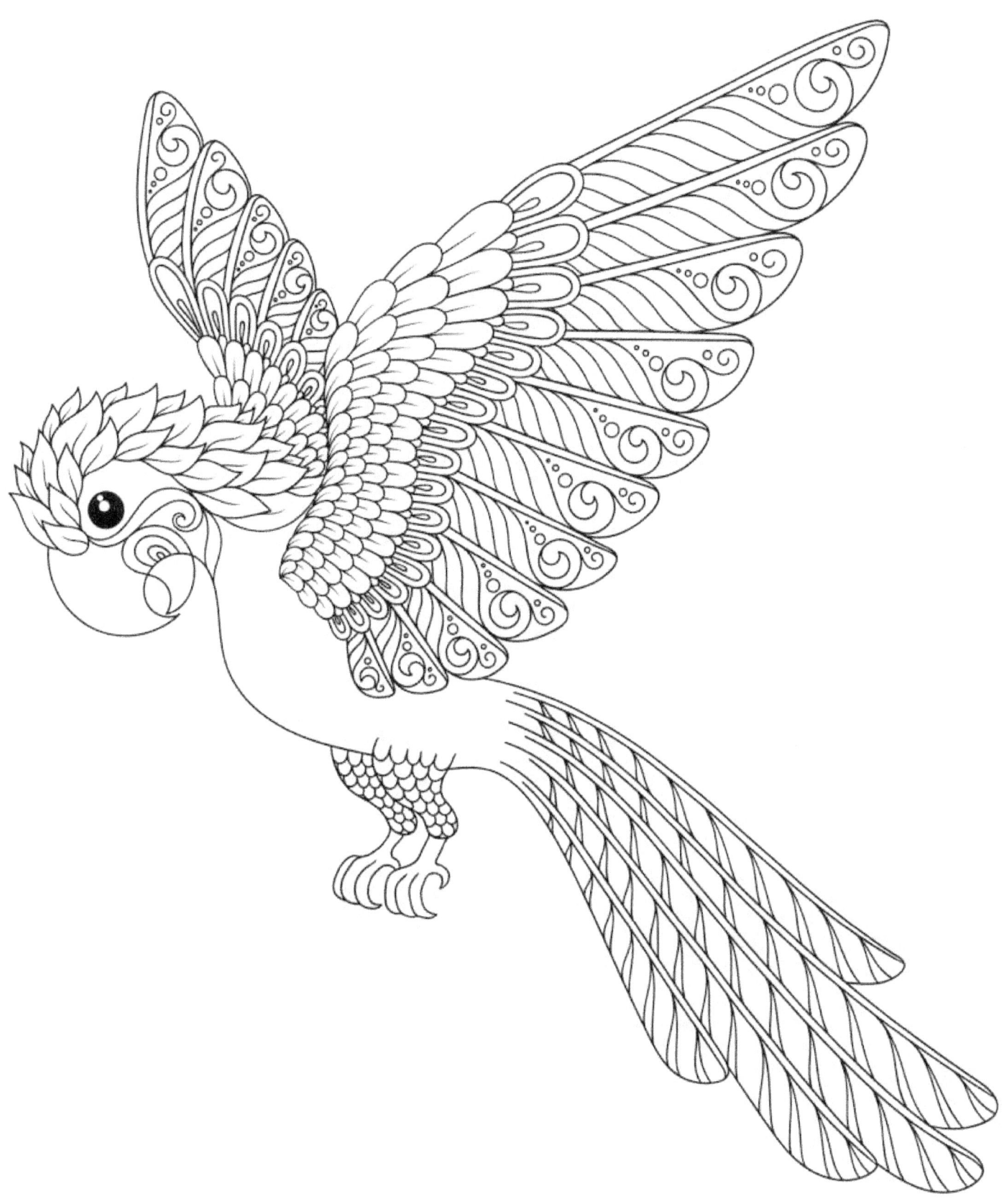

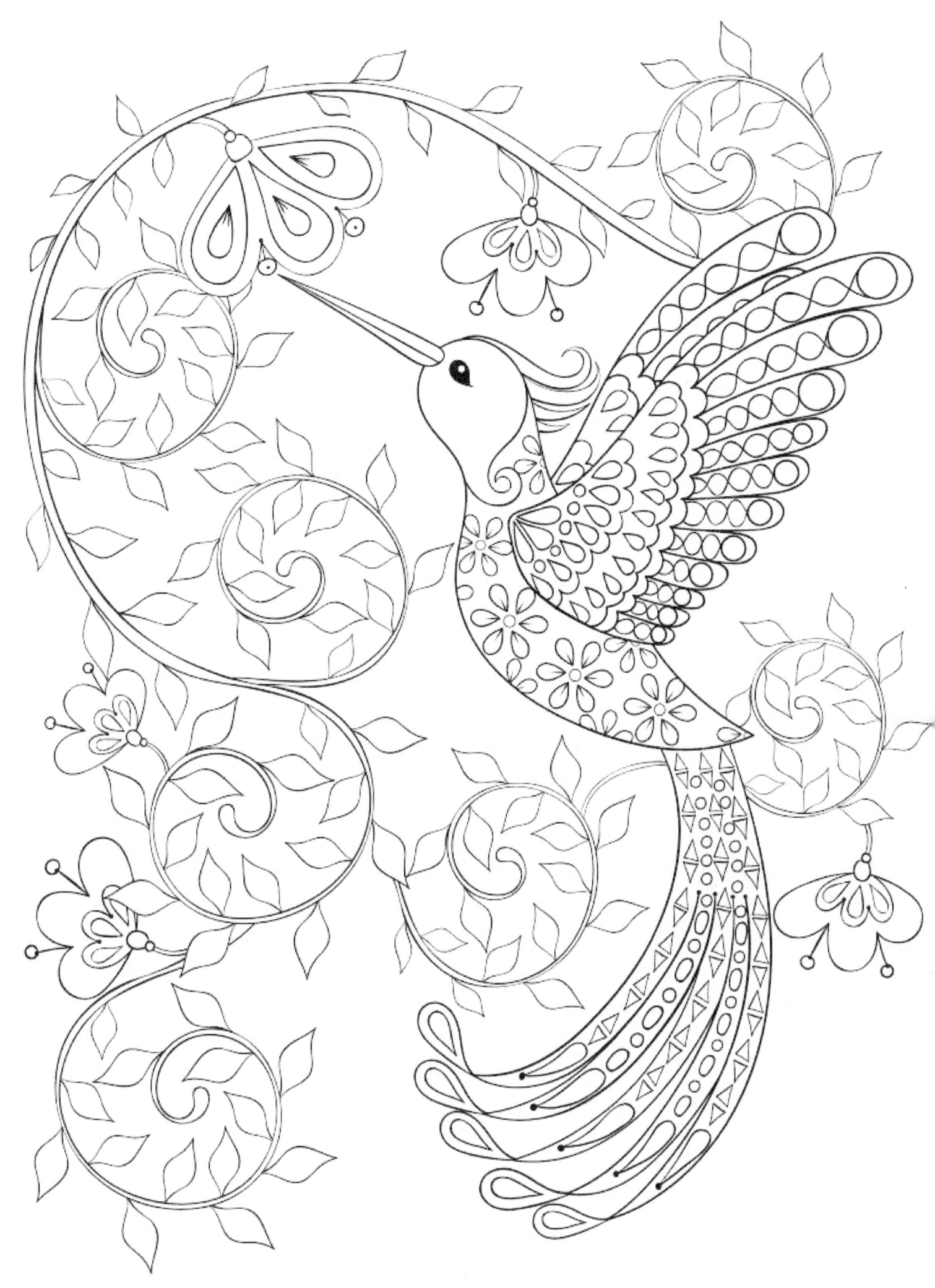

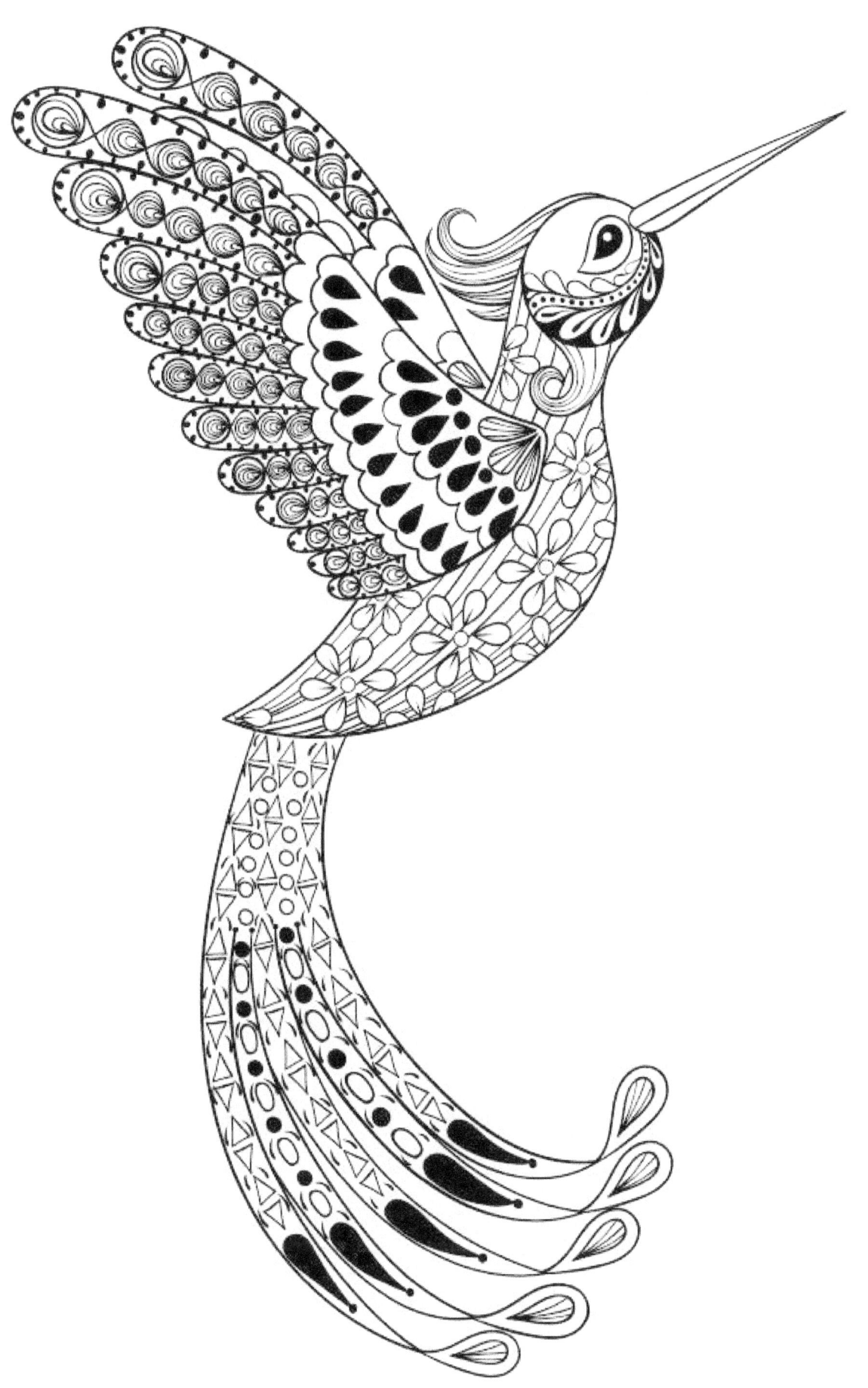

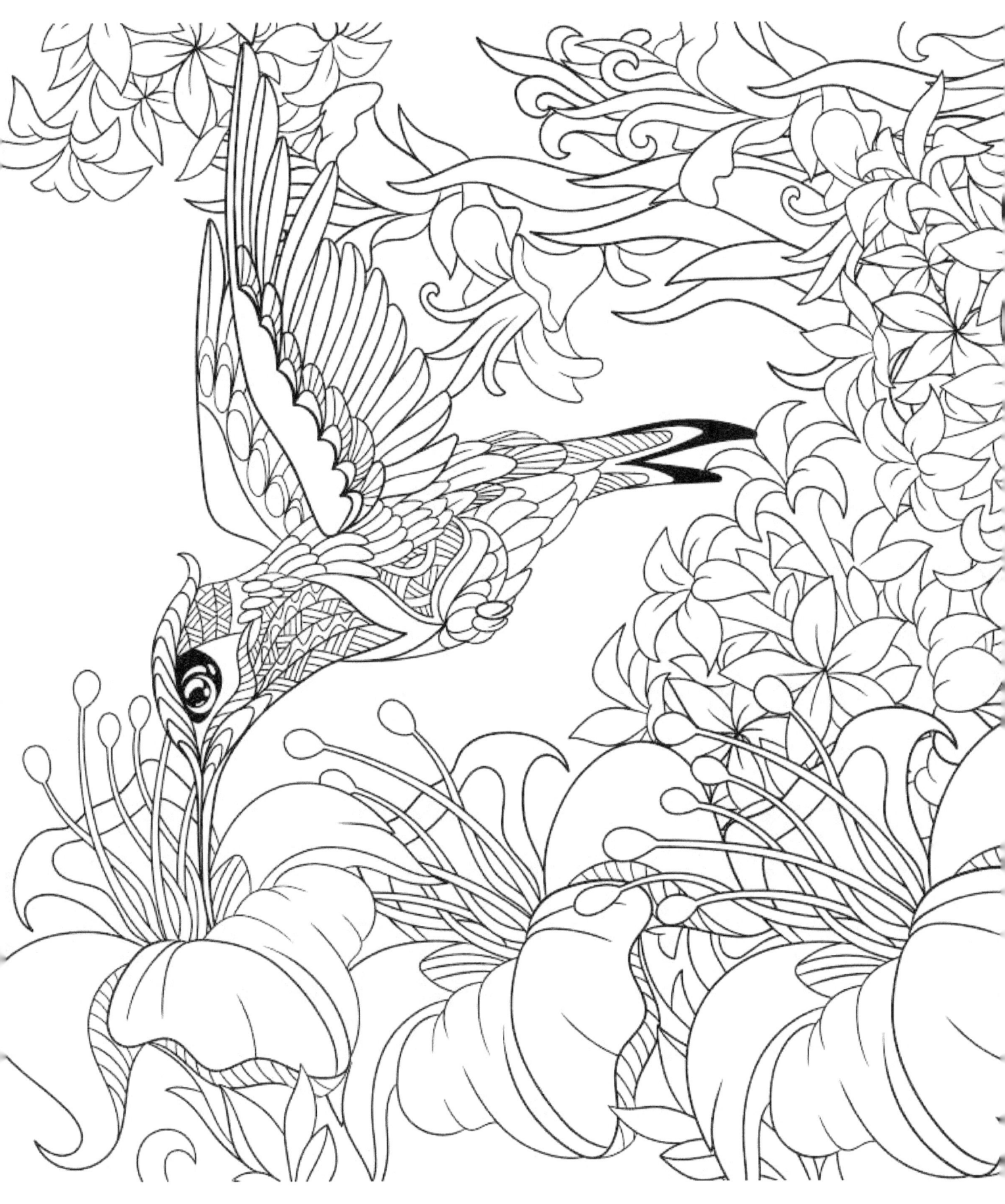

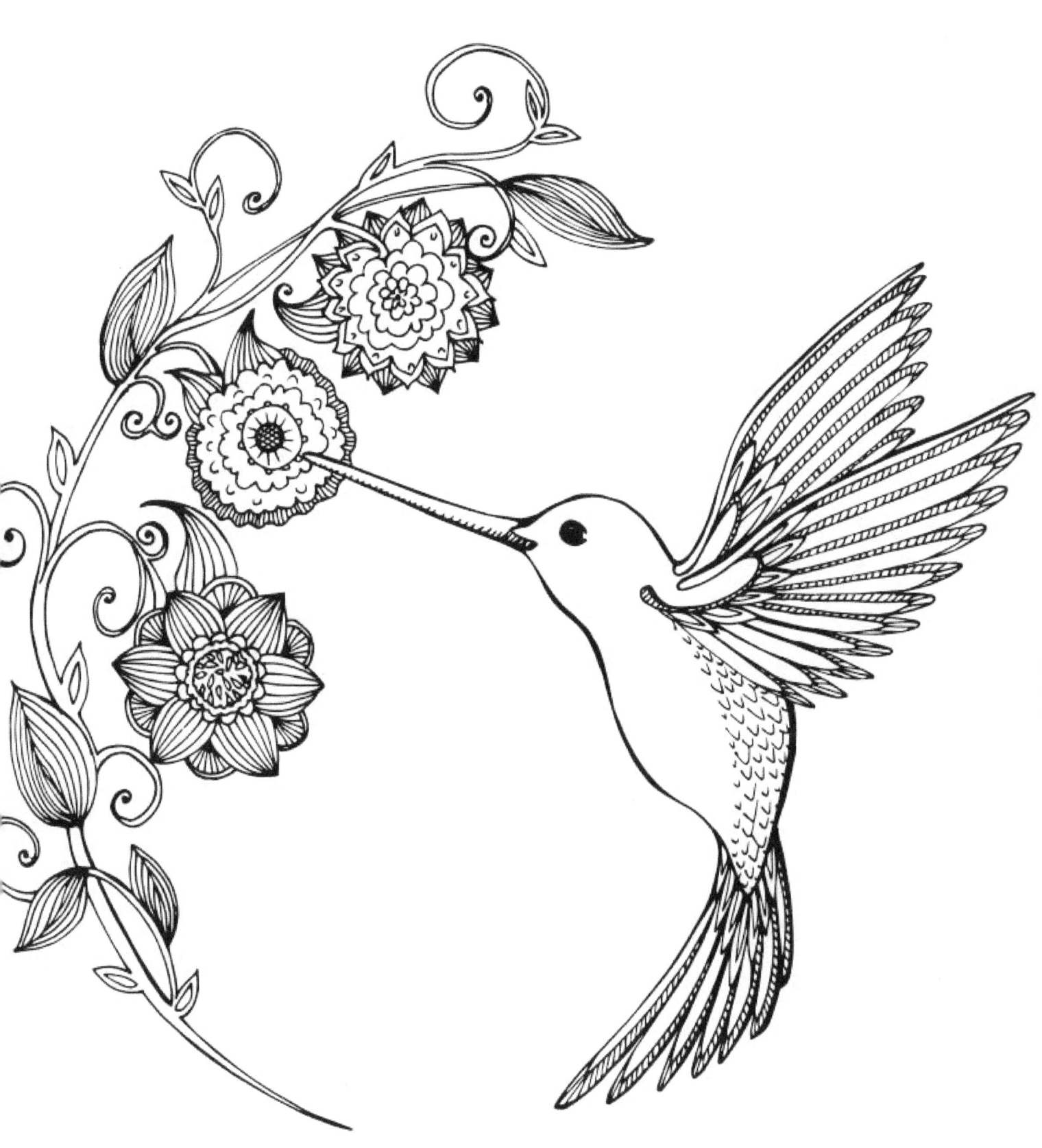

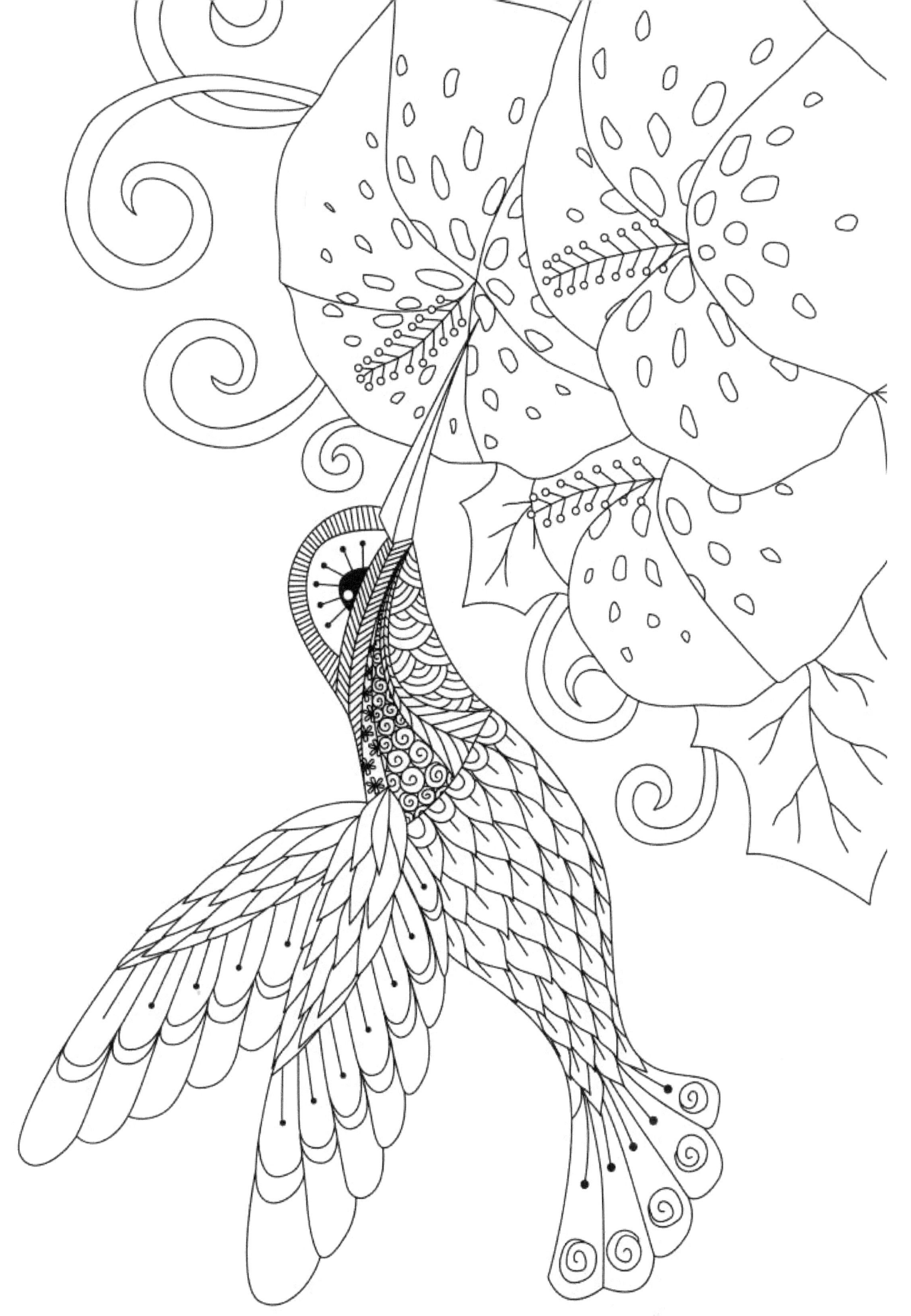

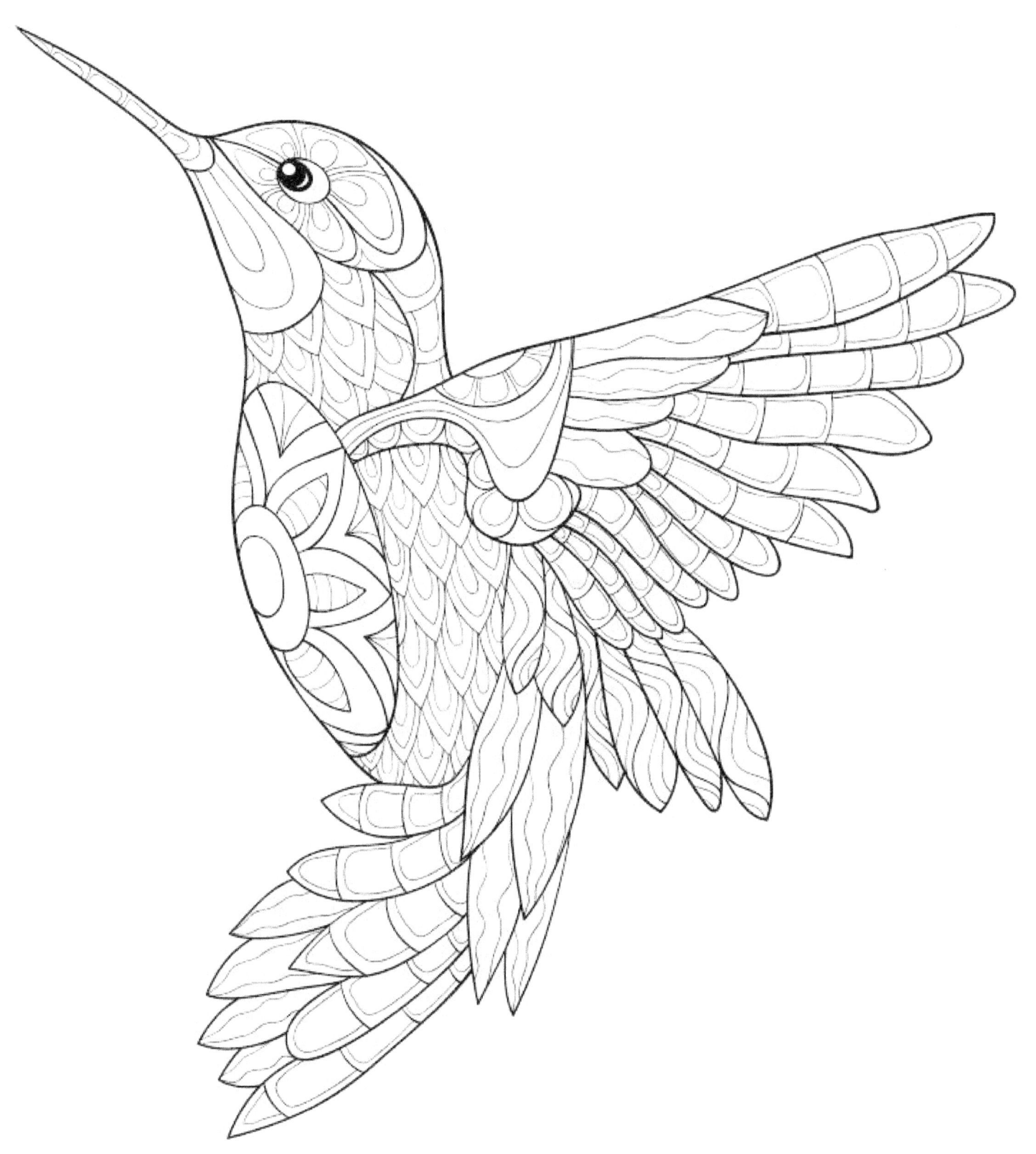

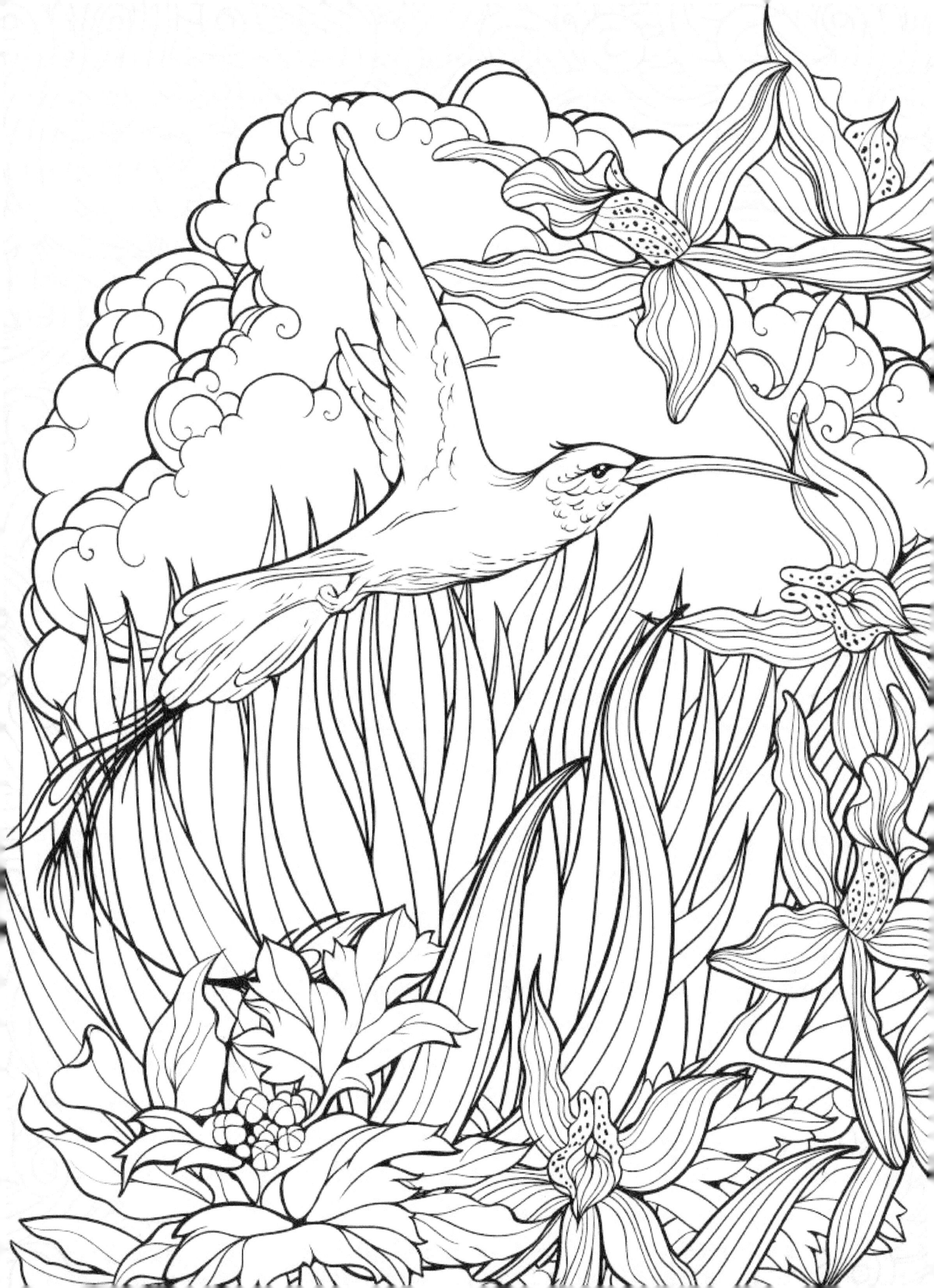

Surprise Bonus Sea Horses Coloring Pages to Enjoy.

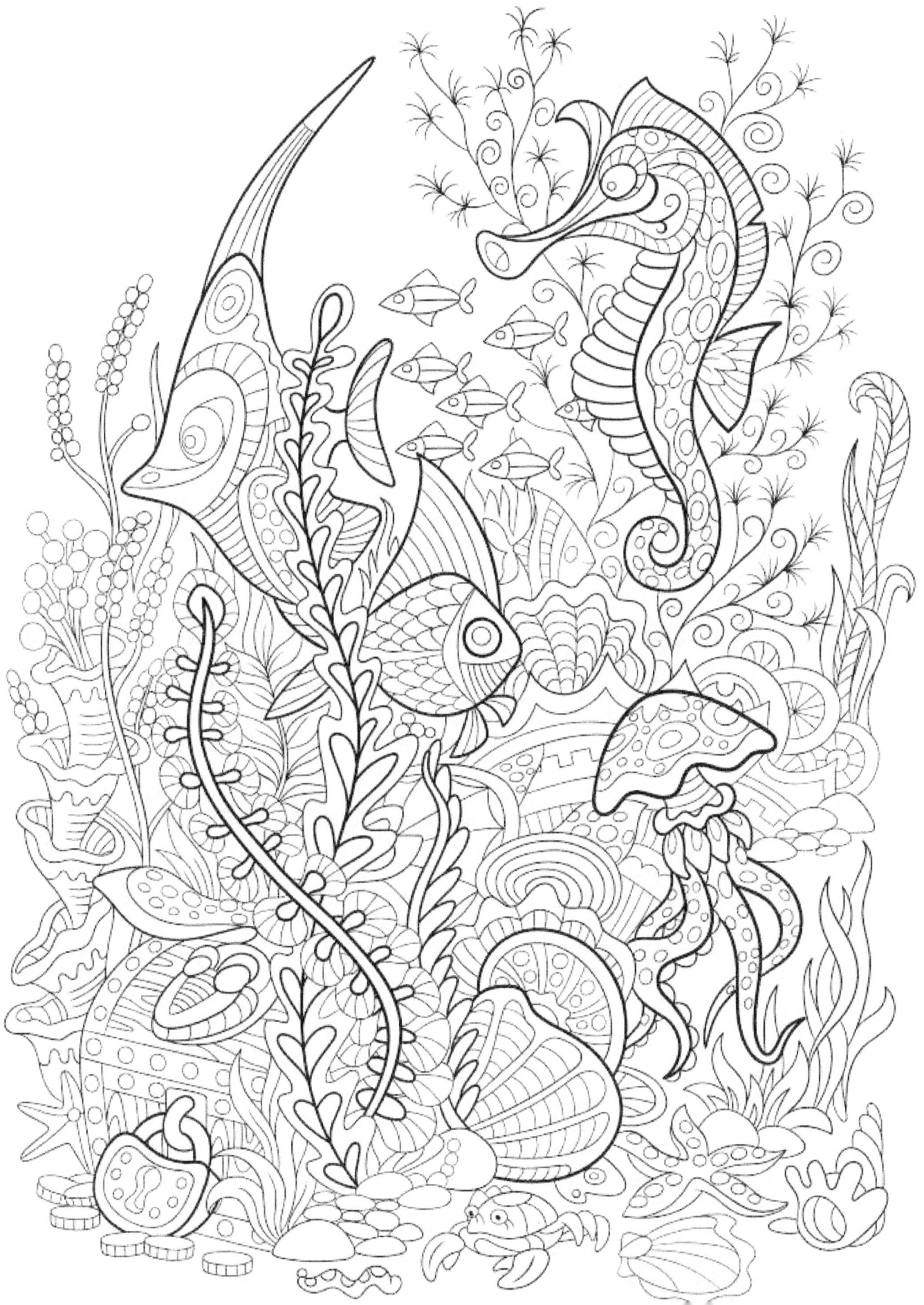

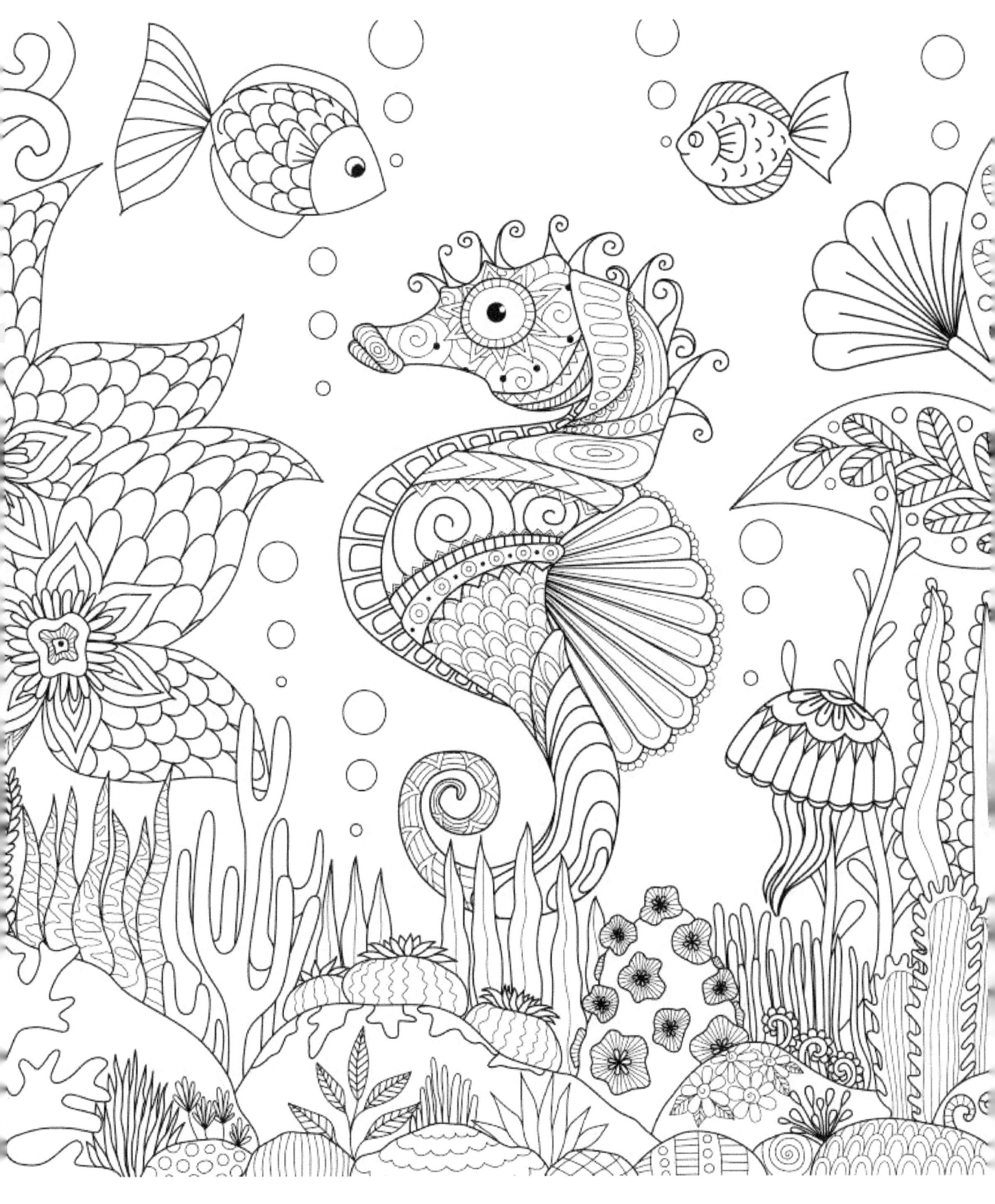

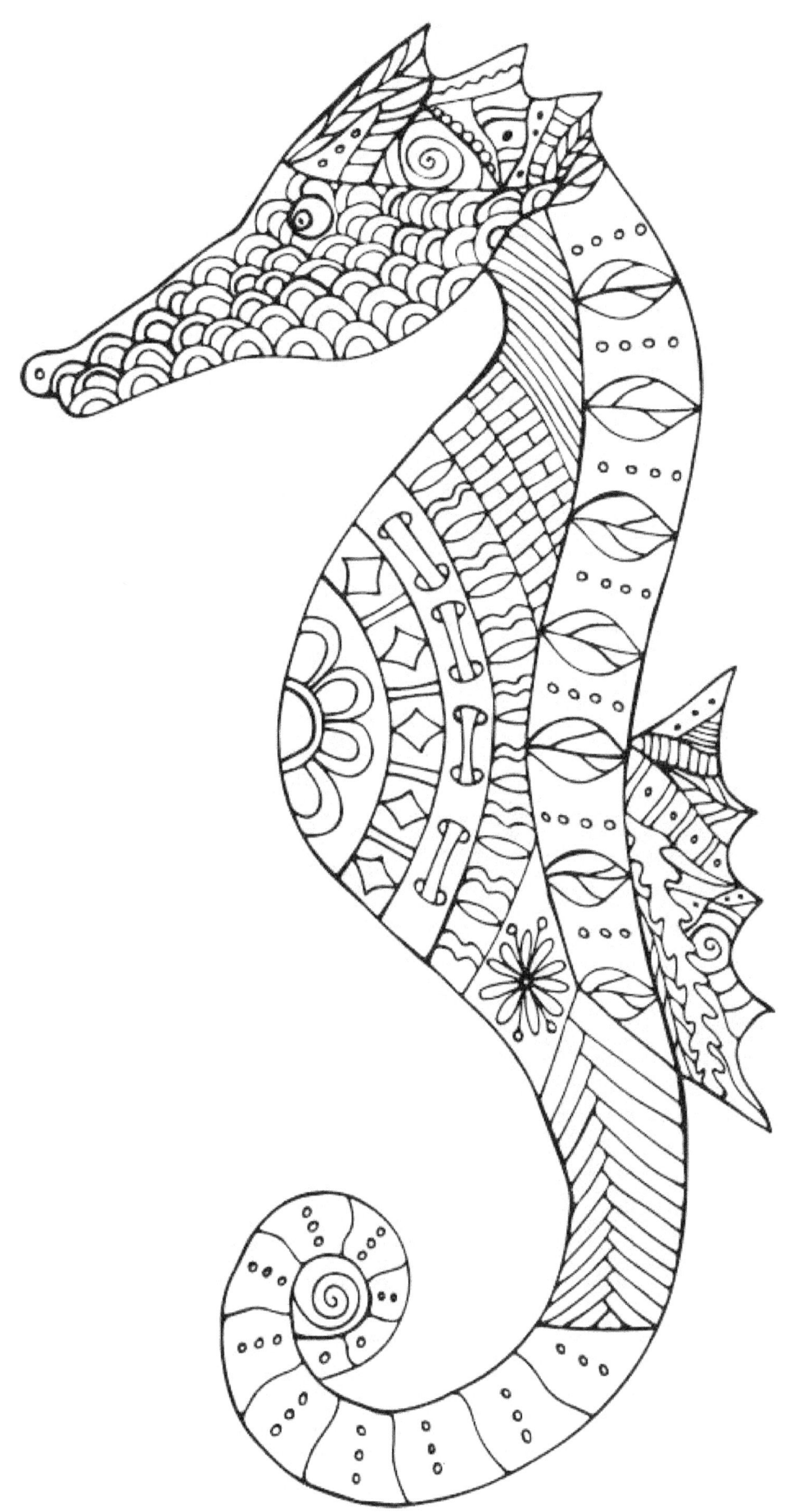

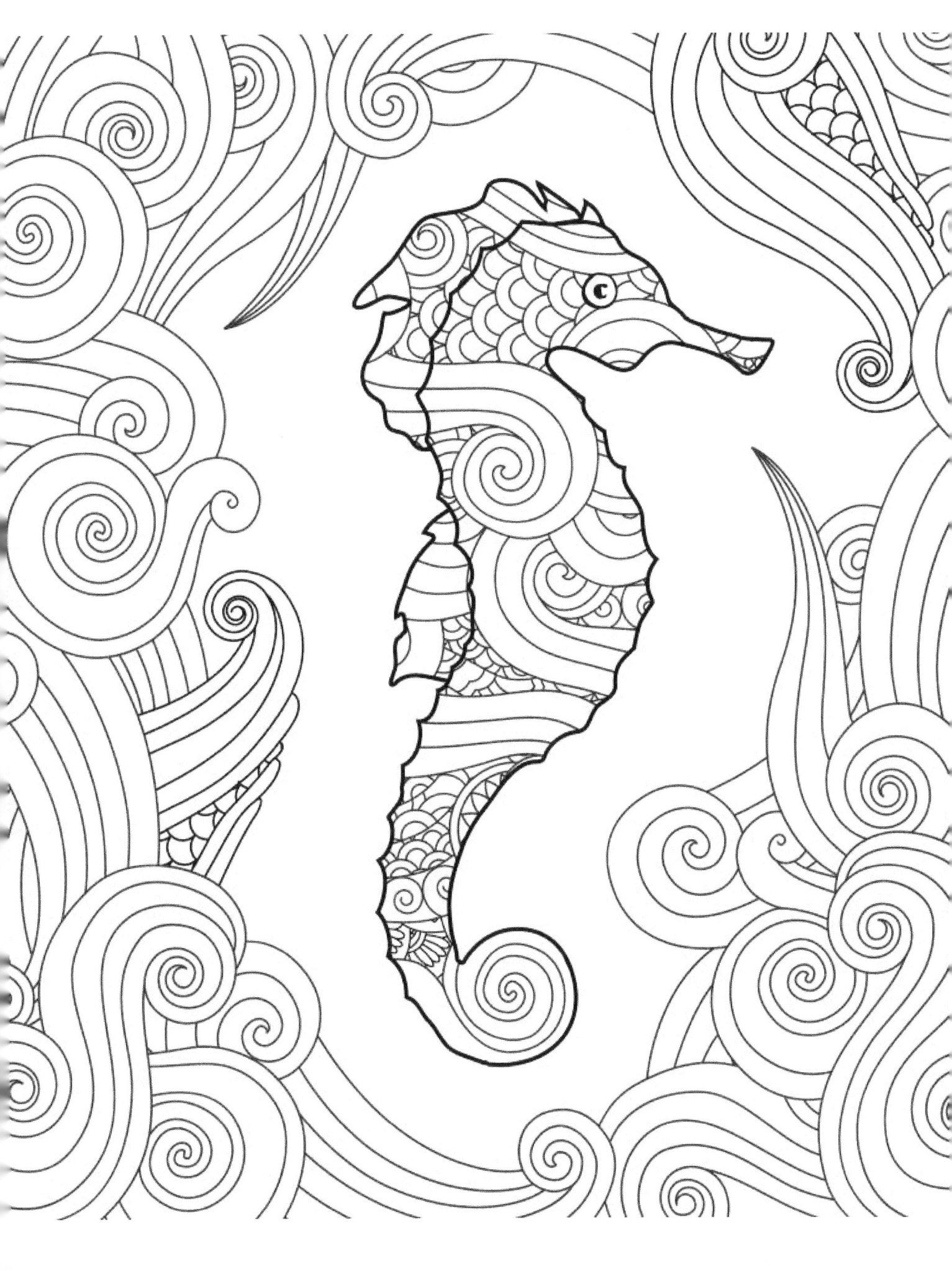

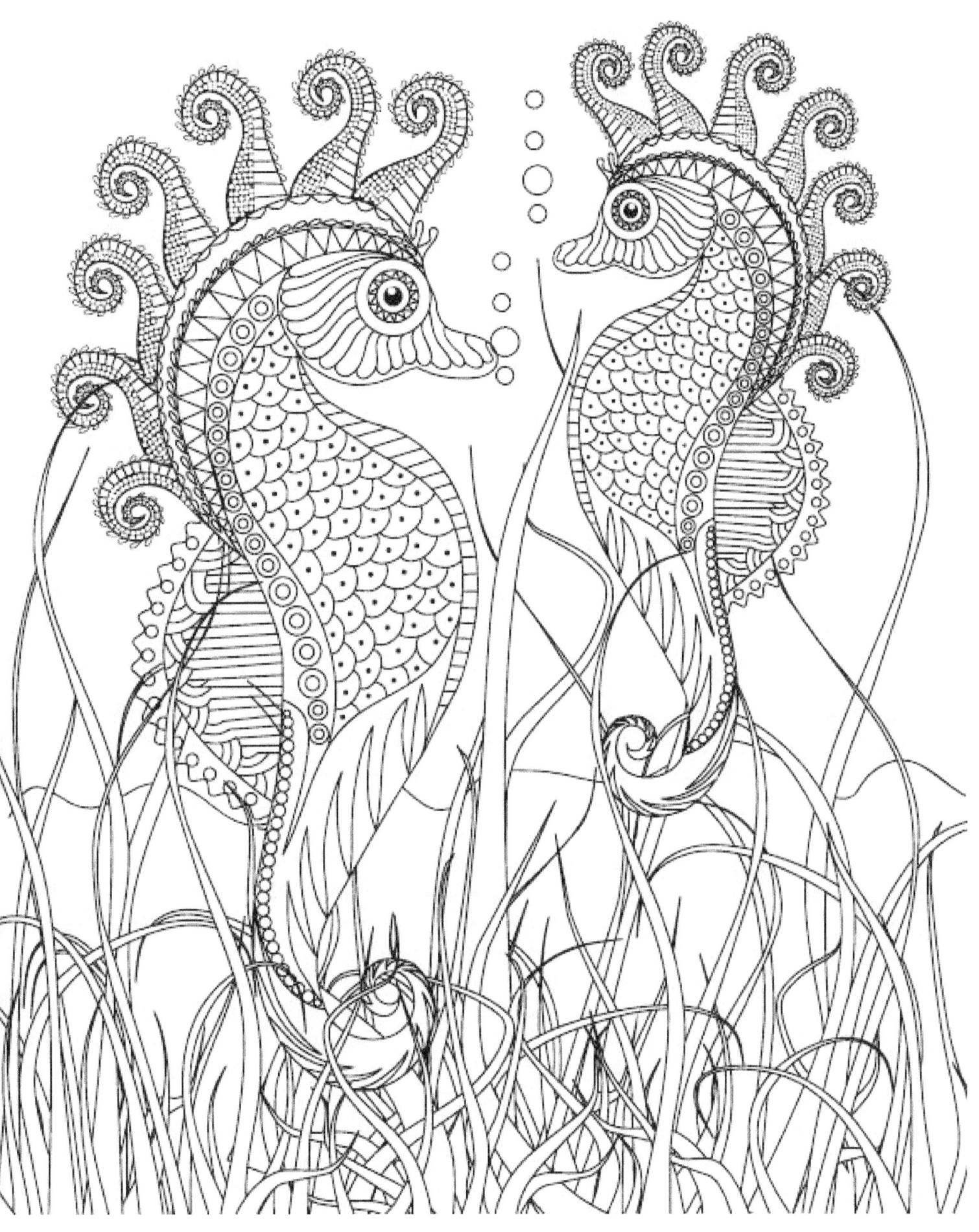

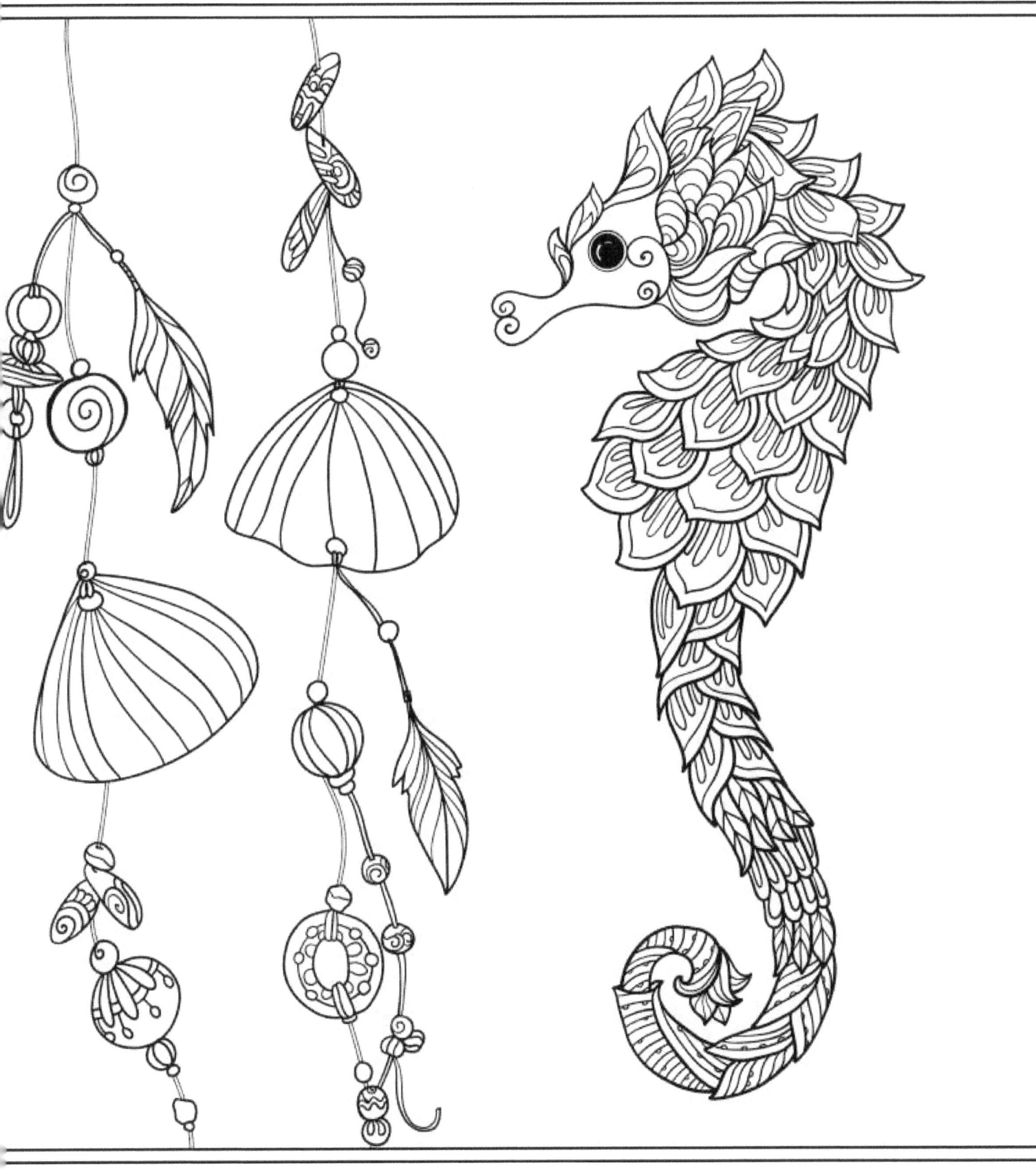

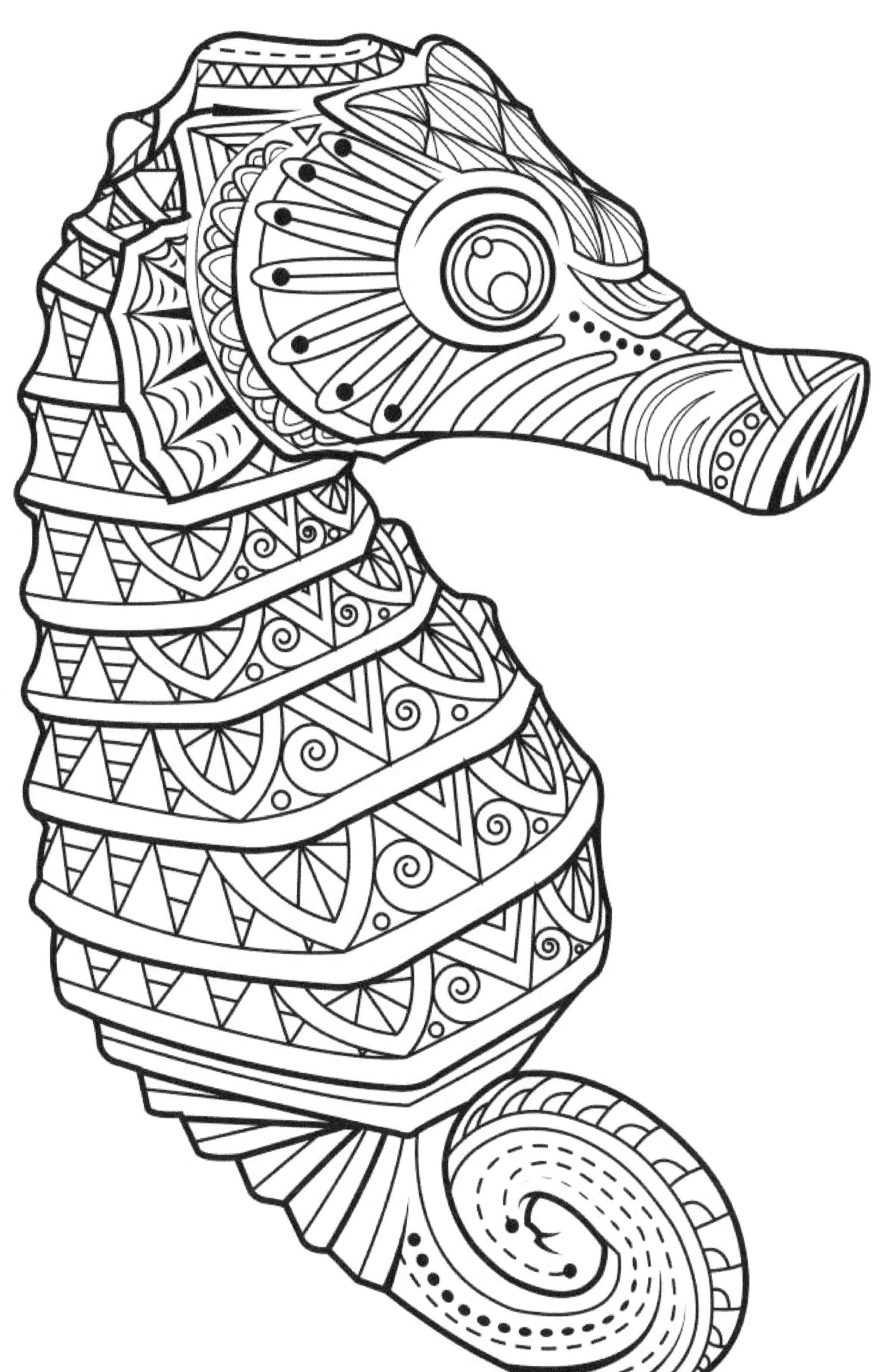

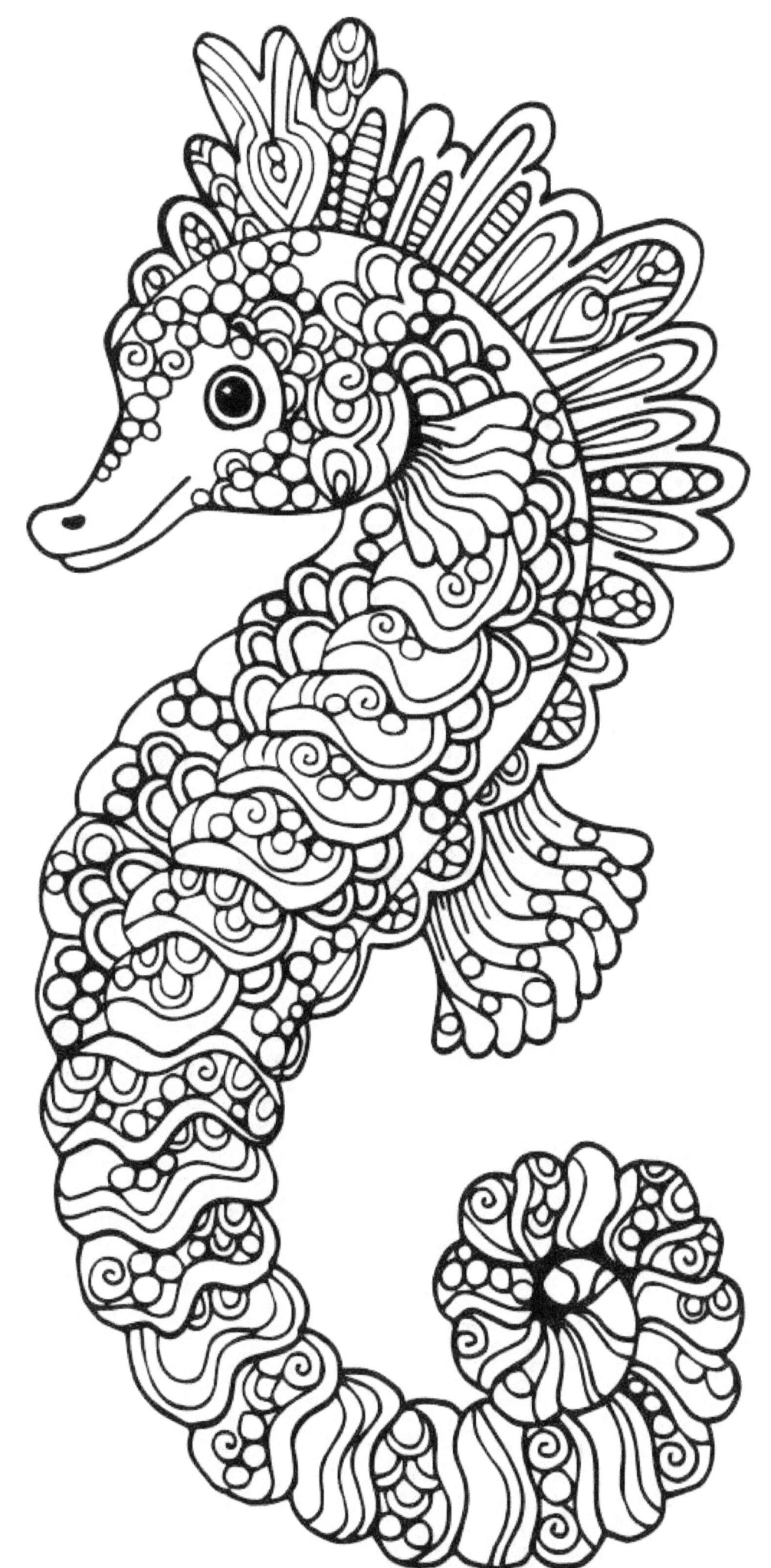

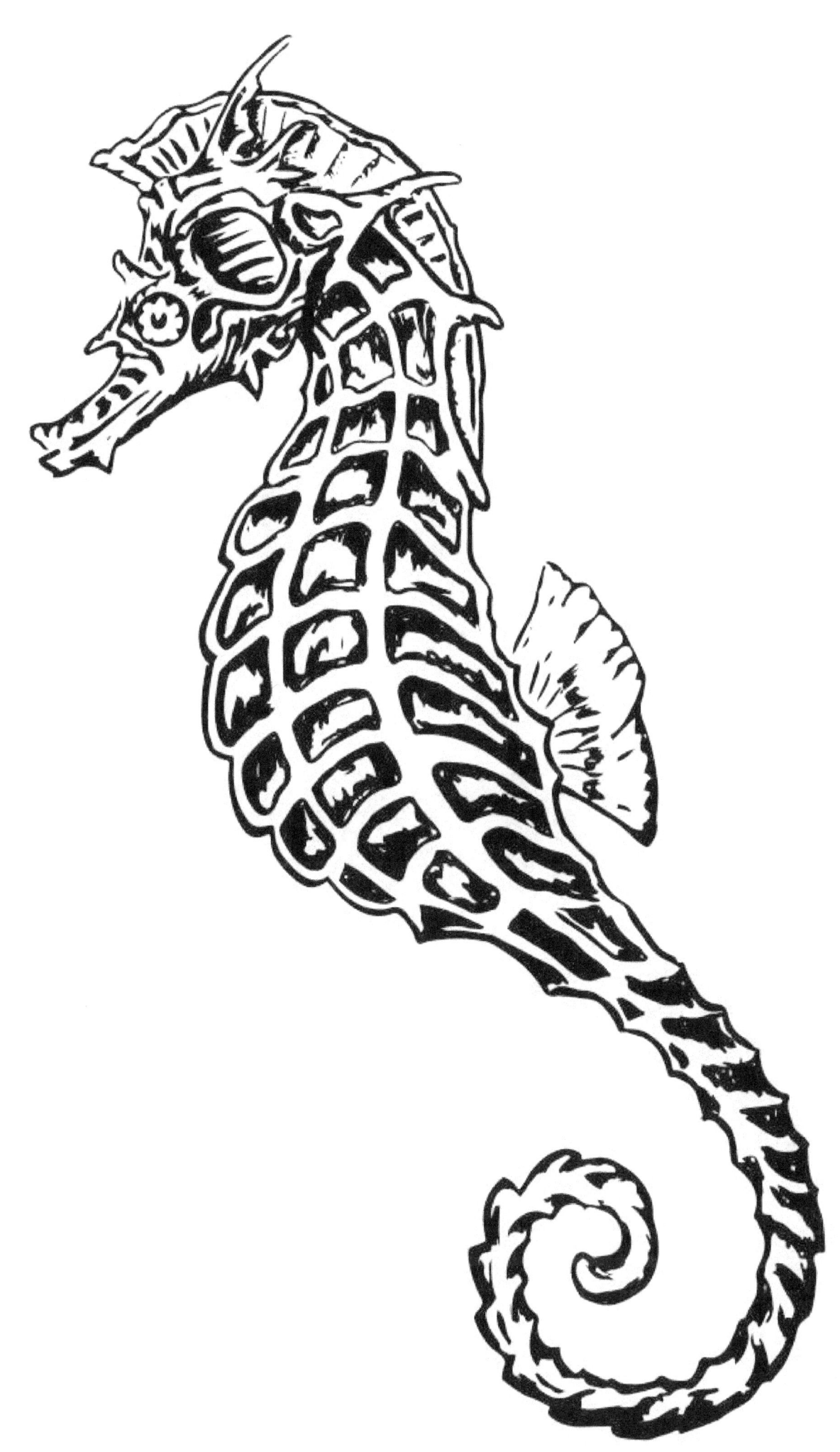

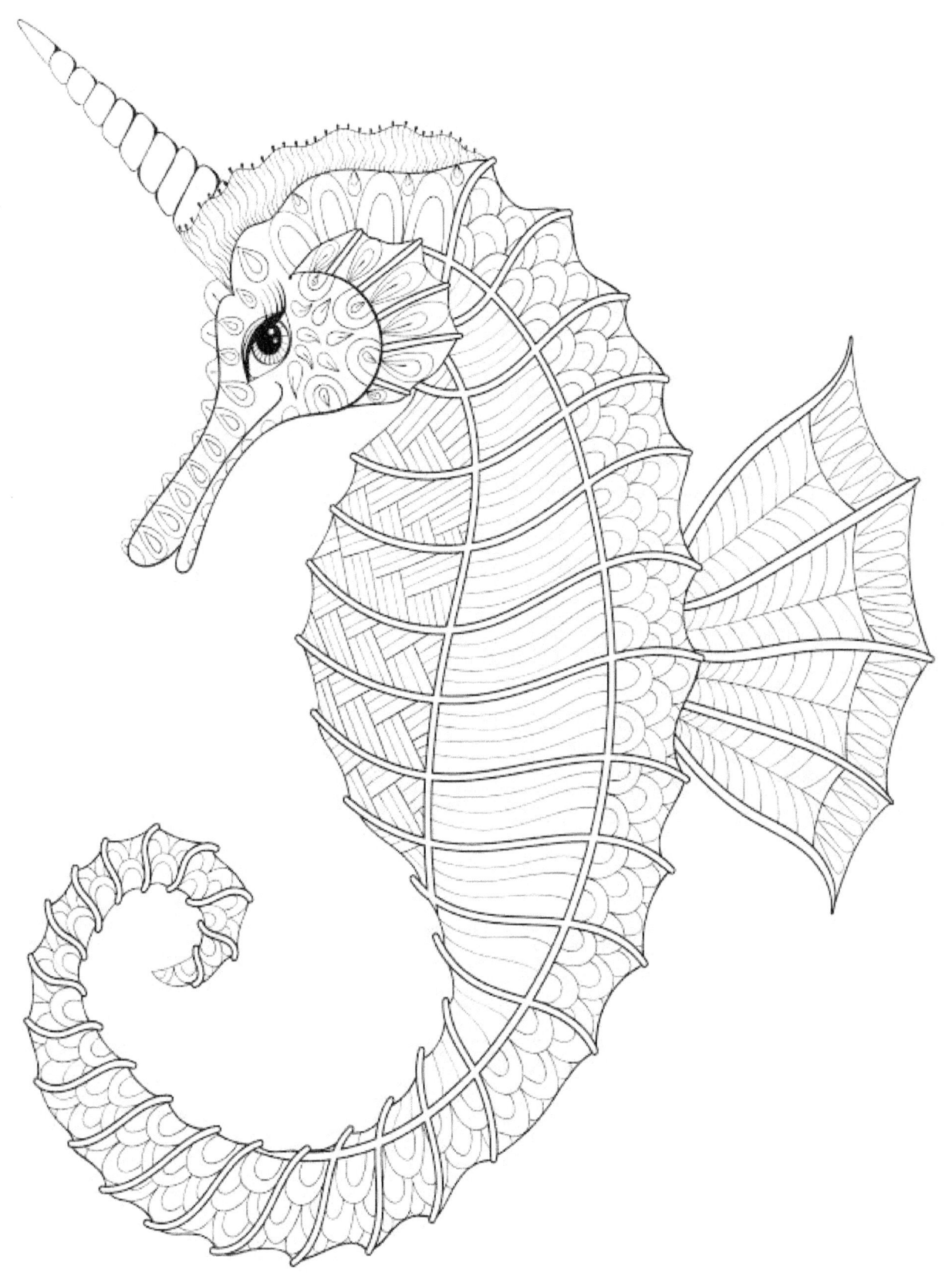

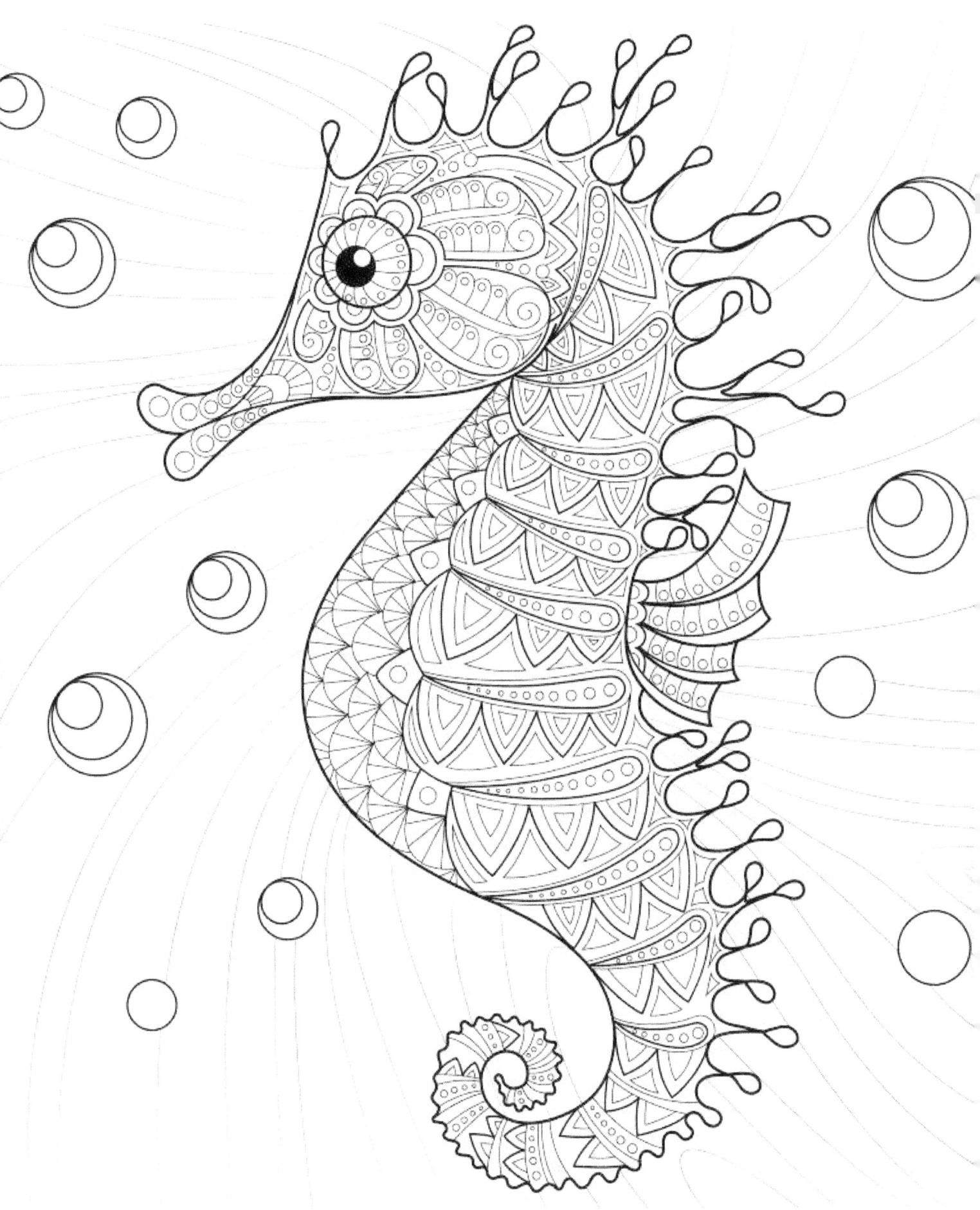

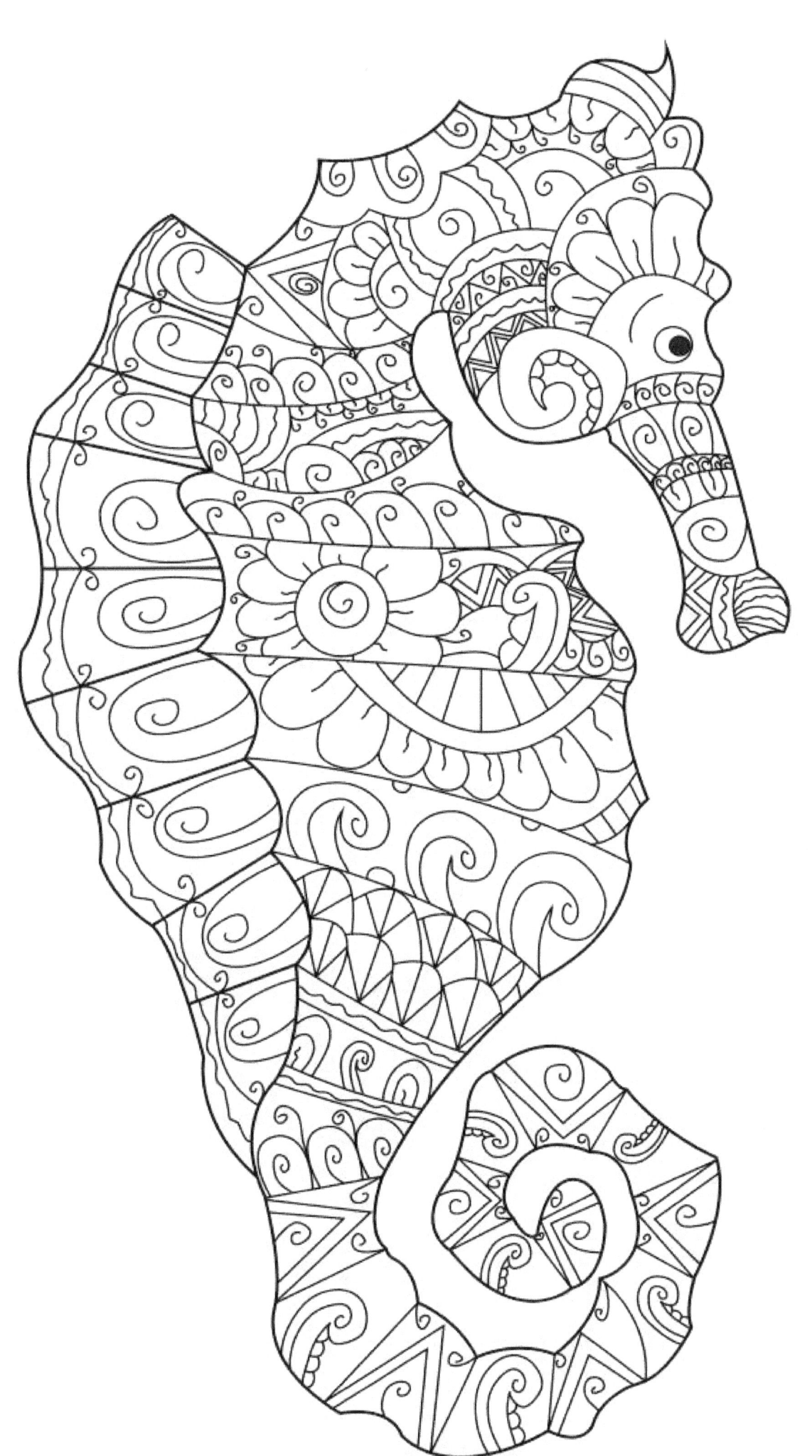

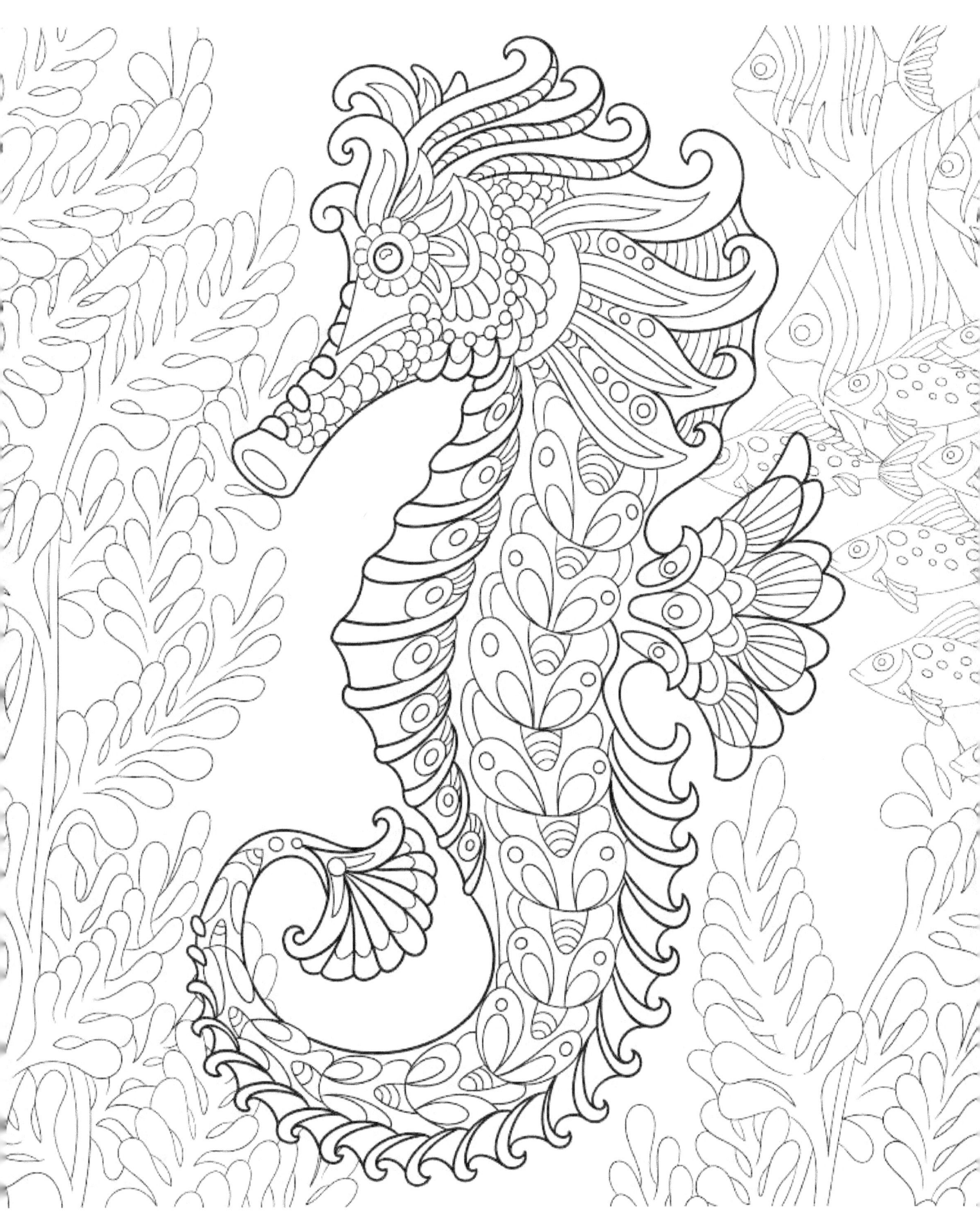

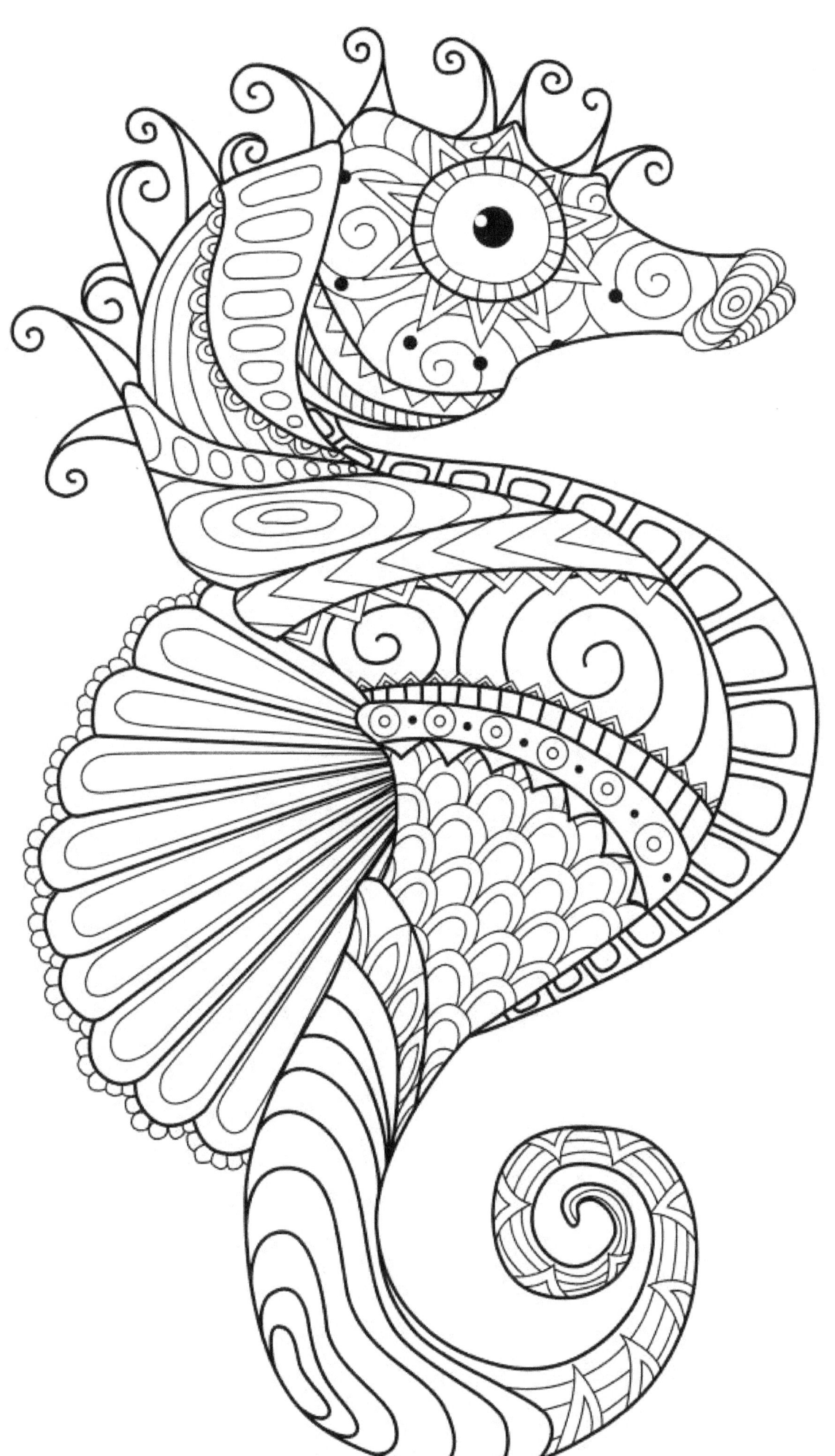

www.ingramcontent.com/pod-product-compliance
Lightning Source LLC
Chambersburg PA
CBHW081224170526
45165CB00009B/2938